Cambridge Elements ≡

Elements in Business Strategy
edited by
J.-C. Spender
Kozminski University

PEOPLE CENTRIC INNOVATION ECOSYSTEM

Japanese Management and Practices

Yingying Zhang-Zhang
International University of Japan

Takeo Kikkawa
International University of Japan

CAMBRIDGE
UNIVERSITY PRESS

Shaftesbury Road, Cambridge CB2 8EA, United Kingdom

One Liberty Plaza, 20th Floor, New York, NY 10006, USA

477 Williamstown Road, Port Melbourne, VIC 3207, Australia

314–321, 3rd Floor, Plot 3, Splendor Forum, Jasola District Centre, New Delhi – 110025, India

103 Penang Road, #05–06/07, Visioncrest Commercial, Singapore 238467

Cambridge University Press is part of Cambridge University Press & Assessment, a department of the University of Cambridge.

We share the University's mission to contribute to society through the pursuit of education, learning and research at the highest international levels of excellence.

www.cambridge.org
Information on this title: www.cambridge.org/9781108986717

DOI: 10.1017/9781108981200

First published 2023

A catalogue record for this publication is available from the British Library.

ISBN 978-1-108-98671-7 Paperback
ISSN 2515-0693 (online)
ISSN 2515-0685 (print)

Cambridge University Press & Assessment has no responsibility for the persistence or accuracy of URLs for external or third-party internet websites referred to in this publication and does not guarantee that any content on such websites is, or will remain, accurate or appropriate.

People Centric Innovation Ecosystem

Japanese Management and Practices

Elements in Business Strategy

DOI: 10.1017/9781108981200
First published online: June 2023

Yingying Zhang-Zhang
International University of Japan

Takeo Kikkawa
International University of Japan

Author for correspondence: Yingying Zhang-Zhang, zhangeles@gmail.com

Abstract: How can knowledge management function well in a highly dynamic VUCA context? This Element focuses on the context of Japanese management and practices to present the concept of people-centric innovation ecosystem. An overview of Japanese management is provided, from publications in English to the insiders' view of Japanese scholars, combining these sources with interviews and dynamic groups with local managers and case studies to illustrate the state and evolution of Japanese management and practices. Highlighting the people-centricity in Japanese management, its networked innovative capability sustains enterprise development in a highly dynamic VUCA context. The interconnectedness and mutual influence of Japanese and Western management have the potential to generate more general management advancements. This Element aims to contribute to the debate on generalization and contextualization, culture and metaculture, and the coexistence of convergence and divergence. Japanese womenomics and its implications for Asian emerging economic powers are also discussed.

Keywords: strategic people management, people centricity, knowledge worker, Japanese management, innovation ecosystem

ISBNs: 9781108986717 (PB), 9781108981200 (OC)
ISSNs: 2515-0693 (online), 2515-0685 (print)

Contents

1 Introduction

In a volatile, uncertain, complex, and ambiguous (VUCA) context, such as the one in which we live, management and organizations are confronted with the challenge of how to perform better. For instance, Softbank could sell its ARM shares to NVIDIA or not depending on the authorities of different countries and regions; Alibaba's share values might halve while its business revenues and margins continue growing; reducing chip production creates a shortage of supply that affects the video game console, PC, and automobile industries. All these examples show that today's political, legal, societal, and business environments are full of uncertainty and interconnectivity. The quote "uncertainty is the only certainty there is," written by mathematician John Allen Paulos (2003) – who, in the words of his father, never played the market and knew little about probability – has been echoed around the world in different contexts.

Due to the ongoing effects of COVID-19, society at all levels is navigating uncertain waters, intending to survive and keep healthy, all the while setting its mind to work in a certain direction. "And knowing how to live with insecurity is the only security" continues Paulos (2003), strategically. The management world is no exception. Long before COVID-19, Spender (2014) already specifies that, contrary to legal definitions, firms and their managers need to deal with buzzing, dynamic activities, ambiguously defined with imprecision and driven by knowledge absences; this vagueness is due partly to an ambiguous past and present and partly to uncertain future possibilities. Similarly, the fallacy of strategic planning and forecasting, ascribable to highly volatile and uncertain environments, leads Teece (2020) to insist on the dynamic capability in VUCA contexts by means of actions – sense, organize, capture, and renew – rather than by forecasting and predicting based on existing strategic patterns.

Highly dynamic business environments constitute a new context that is more VUCA than ever. Dynamism is induced not only by technology, competitive emerging markets, and crises but also by the cross-level, multiple-source factors of these three elements (Zhang-Zhang, Rohlfer and Varma, 2022). The accelerated pace of technological innovation, comprising digitalization, artificial intelligence, big data, and robotics, is transforming traditional sectors like banking and retailing, but rising multinationals from emerging markets are challenging traditional multinationals from advanced economies, too. Management and organizations are at the crossroads of a paradigm shift; COVID-19, as an opportunity and a threat at the same time, may provide time for reflection on business management and theories. In view of the recent call for "humanizing strategy" (Nonaka and Takeuchi, 2021), COVID-19 dramatizes the constraints between strategic planning and human creativity (Zhang-Zhang and Varma, 2020). Reconciliation is needed and is feasible if we place people at the center of the innovation system. While some industries may suffer more than others from the pandemic's impact, being innovative and creating new knowledge seems the only viable option when such an uncontrollable event occurs.

Knowledge and Innovation

Drucker (1993) reckons that knowledge may be the only meaningful resource. Being innovative to create new knowledge seems the ultimate source, or resource, for strategic management to solve the issue of "knowledge absences." Though knowledge per se has existed as long as the history of humanity (Nonaka and Takeuchi, 1995) and innovation has been developed as an independent research field since the 1950s (Fagerberg, Fosaas, and Sapprasert, 2012), Nonaka and his colleagues have irreversibly changed the course of knowledge management (KM) in contemporary organizational theories (Spender, 2013).

There are various thoughts and areas of investigation regarding KM, and knowledge has been fragmentally treated as a philosophical or epistemological matter, as capital, as information, or as an intangible resource at the core of the social organization (Spender, 2013). Using examples ranging from the eighth-century Abbasid project to collect and translate knowledge from around the world into Arabic, to the Penrosian tradition in modern theory, Spender (2013) narrates the shift of KM from its deep-rooted and broad scope to a narrowly framed issue "in terms of the private sector economic and organizational impact of knowledge (or knowing) and its management," segmented according to different disciplines with different axioms (p. 27). Spender ingeniously analyzes the uncertain condition of KM and innovation, considered as production of additional resources "to be administrated and managed as they 'bulk-up' the firm's bundle" (p. 30). He also underlines Nonaka's contribution to the field of KM across different dimensions, albeit acknowledging the success of the KM branch in IT systems, as well as other intellectual alternatives like communities of practice and dynamic capabilities.

Regardless of whether the rise of KM was due to rapid improvements in the cost-effectiveness of computers or to academic interest in how knowledge has an impact on innovation in a globalized world characterized by high-speed technological development (Prusak, 2000; Teece, 2008), the IT system view of KM is only one of the perspectives, even though it has attracted a great deal of investment and attention (Spender, 2013). Above all, to make knowledge or know-how workable and contribute to economic value-adding, people are the source of creative ideas and are generators and convertors of knowledge innovation and learning processes. Zhang, Zhou, and McKenzie (2013) adopt the term "knowledge worker" from Nonaka (1995), while Spender (2014: viii) notes that the individual is at the core of the model for "having powers of imagination and judgment along with powers of logic." In this Element we also follow this approach by placing people at the center of our model (i.e., a people centric innovation ecosystem). Without the creativity and innovation arising from the minds and hearts of individuals, all logic will collapse without meaning in management, just like nice words that stay on paper but are never put into action and turned into reality. While the work of Nonaka and his colleagues on KM is bold and multifaceted, we are especially interested in the humanistic dimension of knowledge creation, which Zhang, Zhou, and McKenzie (2013) refer to as people centric innovation.

People Centric Innovation and Strategically Managing People

We agree with Spender (2014) that, instead of knowledge management being a diversion from strategy, strategic work indeed could be viewed as dealing with "knowledge absences." Hence, a strategy needs to help an organization acquire the competencies and capabilities needed to achieve its goals. Individuals working with knowledge, called knowledge workers (Nonaka, 1995), are at the center of strategic interest to be explored and managed.

At the same time, innovation as knowledge creation emerged and evolved in different phases in modern theory to confront different challenges that organizations faced (Fagerberg et al., 2012). Before 1970, innovation studies were still in their infancy, confining themselves to the fields of economics and sociology; until the late 1980s, innovation attracted the interest of a large number of researchers and it became a global phenomenon of a multi- and interdisciplinary nature, tracing different trajectories; later, it entered its maturity phase, marked by the creation of professional associations and journals focusing on developing this field of inquiry. Organizational innovation gained more research attention after 1990, along with other clusters of innovation studies, namely economics of research and development (R&D) and innovation systems (Fagerberg et al., 2012).

Research diversity in the field of innovation is undoubtedly beneficial for knowledge creation in the scholarly community (March, 2004). However, although the field is relatively mature, no clear, integrated framework has been formulated yet (Mayer, 1999; Zhang, Zhou, and McKenzie, 2013). This provides an opportunity to approach knowledge and innovation from a humanistic perspective to strategically manage people so as to achieve performance-oriented goals (Zhang, Zhou, and McKenzie, 2013). Innovation is highly risky because no positive results can be guaranteed, since managing and strategic work "is highly specific and contextualized, not at all general" (Spender, 2014: viii). Thus, regarding an organization as a platform and context for individuals to create knowledge and disseminate it (Nonaka, 1994) is a meaningful foundation to achieve innovation performance. Simply put, if people and their creativities are not in place, huge investments in IT systems and economies of R&D are of no use for transforming outcomes into commercializable innovative products and fostering their market adoption. The people centric innovative capability is valuable, rare, and difficult to imitate and, if firms can find ways to manage, explore, and exploit it, competitive advantages can then be gained and sustained. In other words, high-performing organizational innovation capabilities depend on processes, structure, motivation, and organizational alignment (Grant, 2013), along with human creativity.

This Element attempts to propose a people centric innovative ecosystem that interrelates people, connecting knowledge generation and management systems across different levels (i.e., individual, organizational, industrial, national, and global) in order to achieve sustainability. We utilize the context of Japanese management and practices for this purpose because Japan was the first Eastern country that challenged the Western economy in the 1970s, and it is still the only advanced Eastern economy in the top positions of global Gross Domestic Product (GDP) ranking. Growing from an emerging economy in the 1950s, the stably developed Japanese organizations are deserving of attention with regard to their achievements and challenges in the current VUCA contexts and digitalization world; not to mention that many Japanese firms have managed to survive and sustain their business through major crises of all kinds over several centuries, and some for more than 1,000 years (Dooley and Ueno, 2020).

Japan and the Rising Asian Emerging Economies

Since World War II, the business world has witnessed the rise of Japan from ashes to the role of the first advanced economy in the East. This occurred in the 1970s, but especially in the 1980s and 1990s, a time that global business called the era of Japanese Challenge, following the era of European Expansion and American Dominance (Grant, 2016). As globalization brings accelerated interconnection and interdependence among countries, firms, and individuals (Guillén, 2001), emerging economies and enterprises increase their power and can influence and counterbalance the existing Western multinationals. Asian emerging economies play a critical role in this process, taking the lead in GDP growth, Foreign Direct Investment (FDI) inflow and outflow, and other rankings, like the upgrading of innovative capabilities (Romei and Reed, 2019).

China and India, along with Japan and Korea, rank in the top ten list of the World Intellectual Property Organization (WIPO) in terms of intellectual property (IP) activity and total IP filing (WIPO, 2021).

Asian emerging markets outperform other emerging countries in Africa, Latin America, and Eastern Europe. Japan, the first Asian country to become an advanced economy and still the first in terms of GDP per capita in Asia, might serve as a role model for benchmarking. Though unquestionably recognized as an advanced economy and often classified as part of the Western multinational or economic system by management scholars and economists, Japan struggled during the early decades of its development in pursuit of innovation and new knowledge creation. By scrutinizing the evolution of Japanese management style and practices, the Asian Emerging Economies (AEE) and their companies may be able to improve their management thinking and learning.

Within the context of Asia's rising economic power, our focus here is principally on the firm level, interacting with other levels to better understand the Japanese way of management, which leads to sustainable competitive performance. The structure and the rationale of the Element are as follows. We first review the existing scholarly understanding of Japanese management and practices from quality academic publications in English (Section 2). We then explore the insights of Japanese scholars and practitioners to provide a comprehensive picture of Japanese management (Section 3). The typical features of the Japanese management style comprise on-the-job training, lifetime employment, a seniority-based work system, and company-based trade unions. Nonetheless, we go further and analyze the underlying environmental contexts over time, distinguished enterprise types, and management practices that, by intertwining Japanese and Western (mainly American) management, lead to the coexistence of paradoxical effects and convergence/divergence paths. In Section 4, we provide further qualitative data, via interviews and dynamic groups with Japanese middle-level managers and young professionals, to delve deeper into the issue. The complexity of managing a crisis such as the Fukushima nuclear accident is also critically analyzed. In addition, we describe cases from the Japanese video game industry to offer insights into interconnectivity among people, firms, and industries. Finally, we propose a people centric innovation ecosystem, outlining the innovation ecosystem trends, people centric Japanese management, and practices in Section 5, followed by discussions and conclusions in Section 6. We believe that this theorization is relevant for enterprises in Asian emerging markets, especially for Chinese management, Asian Tigers, and those from the ASEAN-5 countries (i.e., Indonesia, Thailand, Malaysia, the Philippines, and Vietnam) (Cavusgil, Ghauri, and Akcal, 2013), which, in spite of their differences, have certain cultural similarities.

2 Literature Review: What Is Understood as Japanese Management?

Since our interest is to analyze the people centric innovative ecosystem based on the Japanese management context, we would first like to explore what Japanese management and practices are. How do Japanese enterprises grow to be resilient in the global business scenario and come to be regarded as challengers by their Western counterparts? What has brought them to the center of this global stage? What have Westerners learned from Japan and how have they incorporated Japanese management and practices into their mainstream paradigm and renewed themselves?

There have been numerous scholarly publications, both books and journal articles, on this topic. To understand their magnitude, we did a search for "Japanese Management" in Google Scholar on February 8, 2021 and found about 3,780,000 results. An alternative search for "Japan*" and "manag*" in the Web of Science (WoS) database was carried out in 2020 and updated on February 8, 2021, yielding 73,287 results. Due to the large amount of output and the fact that a search test with "Japan* manag*" gave the same number of results, we narrowed our search field down to the titles in the WoS Core Collection, including only management and business as categories, articles as type of document, and English as language, and repeated the process on November 6, 2021. Consequently, the final results provided a more accurate view, focusing on Japanese management discussions among Western business and management scholars, with 181 articles covering the period from 1961 to 2021 (see Figure 1). Based on this, we expanded the relevant scholarly works, using the snowball method starting from the identified publications. This section relies on the preceding semisystematic literature review to investigate the understanding of Japanese management in the major high-quality, English-language academic journals from a Western viewpoint, regardless of whether the authors are from Japan or not.

What Is Japanese Management?

Drucker (1971) clearly states that Japanese managers do business in a distinct fashion from US and European managers, employing different principles, approaches, and policies to tackle problems. The combination of these features was certainly a major factor in the rise of Japanese economy and business. In Westney's (2020) relatively recent overview of Japan's influence on management theory, four management fields are identified that have enjoyed a large contribution from Japanese management: organization behavior/organization studies, production and operations management, strategy, and international

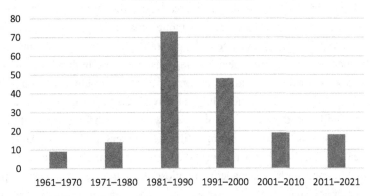

Figure 1 WoS journal publications on Japanese management by period

business (IB). Keeping in mind the discretion of each scholar in categorization, we can generally agree that Japanese management has played a strong role in the area of production and operations (e.g., just-in-time, total quality management and *kaizen*), as well as in managing people (namely human resources or talents), labor-related issues (e.g., lifetime employment, seniority-based reward, and promotion), and organization behavior/organization studies. These aspects are commonly regarded as the typical Japanese style of management and have contributed to both theoretical development and business practices, extending further to the fields of strategy and international business. The contribution to the field of international business has been especially evident, as the variation of the Eastern style of management has been brought into the thinking of predominant Western management thanks to empirical data on Japanese overseas operations and comparative studies between Japanese firms and those of the West, like America and Britain, in addition to the later-rising emerging markets (e.g., Korean, Chinese, and Indian). The contribution to the field of strategy has been more profound, exemplified by the foundation of knowledge schools based on Japanese studies.

The early interest of Westerners in Japanese management was connected to Japanese productivity growth and its relation to the management of employees (Westney, 2020). Dunphy (1987) recognizes Veblen (1915) as the earliest Western commentator that saw Japanese enterprises as different and set up the ensuing debate about Japanese organizational life. Informed by the practices of Japanese managers, Mroczkowski and Hanaoka (1989) present the continuous evolutions and crises of Japanese management, consisting in adjustments to new economic, social, and competitive priorities, from the rigid status promotion in the era prior to World War II, to the labor shortages of the 1950s and 1960s and the peak development of what the world regards as Japanese management in the 1970s. Following this evolutionary logic, we present our review in the same way.

When Arnold (1961) assesses Koichi Inoue's management appraisal system, with its typical Japanese manner of operation, it covers a wide range of management fields. Several peculiarly Japanese traits are highlighted: personnel management centers on future business perspectives rather than on maintaining company competitiveness; high employee performance without waste is pursued; while production is emphasized with an imbalanced attention to control, budgeting, and accounting utilization in comparison to American management. On the other hand, neglected areas in Japanese management are sales and finance. Inoue's management philosophy is indeed viewed as "90 percent personnel management," namely the management of managers and employees, and as seeking systems particular to the individual company.

Early Japanese Management Research

Arnold's assessment (1961) explores a large portion of Japanese-style management, stressing the individual/people as the center of management. Concerning the weak area of marketing, in which Japanese firms struggled, Froomkin (1964) argues that this is due to difficulties in drawing top management's attention and appointing a talented leader to handle these issues. For Froomkin, the decision to apply the Japanese style to American business is questionable because of contextual differences. The heavy presence of traditionalism, seniority, and permanent employment in the career development of Japanese leaders creates a strong corporate environment or culture, centralization of decision-making power, and hierarchical and formal communication styles. Such practices keep up morale, while the rapid growth of Japanese companies provides opportunities for young employees, balancing the formal and hierarchical process for career progress and aligning agency interest with job security.

Along with the preceding characteristics of Japanese management, the *ringi* decision-making system is probably considered the strongest traditional Japanese management practice (Noda and Glazer, 1968). *Ringi* is similar to the American expression "consensus decision-making," but its underlying issue has to do with the quality of personnel/people management in the process when executives invite proposals or comments from lower-level subordinates.

The Evolution of the 1970s and People-Related Factors

After the introductory period of the 1960s, the study of Japanese management grew steadily in the following decade, expanding its comprehension based on the foundations of production and people management, though many works could be classified as belonging to the IB field. Some early examples include Drucker's research (1971) on learning from Japanese management for decision-making and other managerial issues; England and Lee's comparison (1971) of American, Japanese, and Korean cultural impact on managerial values expressed in organizational goals; Fujita and Karger's demonstration (1972) of R&D management in Japan; and Kelley and Reeser's study (1973) of Japanese-American managers' attitudes linked to their Japanese ancestry. England and Lee (1974) continue their comparative study of managerial values in Japan, the United States, India, and Australia, while Johnson and Ouchi (1974)[1] comment on Japanese management taking root in America. Key scholarly works of the late 1970s dealt with Japanese participative management practices (Kuniya and Cooper, 1978), personnel management and employee attitudes (Pascale, 1978), and Japanese multinational operations with regard to the sources and means of control (Hayashi, 1978a).

Drucker (1971) and Johnson and Ouchi (1974) are the two top-cited scholarly pieces of the decade. Both are of a comparative nature and focus on what the West can learn from Japanese management. Drucker (1971) highlights features such as effective decisions, young professional development, and harmony between employment security and other needs, such as productivity, flexibility in labor costs, and change acceptance. Some remarks made by Drucker concern the Japanese propensity to thoroughly define the question before placing emphasis on the answer to increase effectiveness rather than efficiency in problem solving, as well as the crucial role of the "godfather" in a young professional's career development. Moreover, the lifetime employment policy is combined with labor flexibility to balance the economic needs of employees during different phases and to achieve psychological security. In the analysis by Johnson and Ouchi (1974), the exploration of Japanese and US comparative cases raises the question of which elements are standard, universal management practices (Japanese practices already part of Western companies' procedures), which are peculiar to Japanese management and inseparable from Japanese culture (unsuitable for adoption in the United States), and which Japanese approaches and features are exportable (Japanese management that may be transplanted to the United States). Five exportable Japanese management style traits are identified by Johnson and Ouchi: a bottom-up process of information and initiative flow (versus the Western tradition of authority and hierarchy); a top manager as facilitator for decision-making (versus leader-set objectives and orders); a middle manager as molder to coordinate, make the

---

[1] Johnson changed his last name to Pascale, his original family name, in the mid-1970s (Westney, 2020).

complex web of a Japanese organization's relationships work, and get things done (versus the American manager, who rarely coordinates well, lacks human skills, and is less familiar with other parts of the organization); consensus for decision-making (versus individualistic, quick decision-making equated with efficiency); and concern for the personal well-being of employees (versus the American manager's attention to work performance).

The main commonalities among these two top-cited articles and other research of the period are implicit or explicit learning from the best practices of Japanese management, with the intent to apply them to the Western context. Scholars have largely attributed Japan's success to people-related factors, including the nation's highly industrious and homogeneous workforce, constructive relationships with the labor unions, an environment of not encouraging job mobility between companies, more resources spent on nonpayroll benefits per employee, and employees with a stronger perception of satisfaction (Pascale, 1978).

Similarly, other scholars, like Kuniya and Cooper (1978), point out that Japan is known for its comparatively greater potential in improving the quality of working life (not firm performance) through increased shop floor involvement in decision-making, work redesign experiments, and so on. They conclude that this potential is due to various historical and cultural factors, with greater worker participation and more work humanization projects.

The Period of Booming Research on Japanese Management

Managerial interest in Japanese management in the West, including the United States, was at its peak in the 1980s and early 1990s (Makino and Lehmberg, 2020; Westney, 2020), as confirmed by the large increase in academic publications during this period, shown in Figure 1. The understanding of what Japanese management is was consolidated and further expanded in the 1980s, when scholarly works also paid more attention to systematically reviewing and understanding Japanese management. This increased attention, however, was not without criticism, and most scholars still explicitly or implicitly compared Japanese management with American management, also extending the comparison to management in other countries, both in the West (e.g., British management) and in the East (e.g., Chinese, Singaporean, and Korean management). Internationalization context studies, analyzing either Japanese overseas subsidiaries or international businesses in Japan, also multiplied thanks to the protracted business expansion of Japanese multinationals.

Japanese Management of Innovation

As product innovation is a key success factor for Japanese multinationals in the worldwide business, innovation is worthy of exploration. Advancing Fujita and Karger's descriptive exposition (1972) of Japanese research and development, Gerstenfeld and Sumiyoshi (1980), Maruta (1980), and Prochaska (1980) investigate innovation management further. While Maruta addresses *tetsuri* as the Japanese philosophical approach, with principles and guidelines to apply to general and R&D management, Gerstenfeld and Sumiyoshi, as well as Prochaska, more practically compare Japanese management and American management styles in terms of differences in managing innovation.

Prochaska (1980) attempts to understand why and how Japanese companies manage successful innovation through the arguments of a homogenous society, profit and survival, customer orientation, personal and business risk, organization and decision-making, and job experience. Recognized as an island culture and a unified country, Japan learns to cope with problems in its own way. Operating in a homogeneous and collective society, Japanese businessmen tend to take a broader approach when evaluating alternatives. This drives a vision to achieve an extremely high level of stable employment so as to productively use the people on the payroll, as well as to prioritize long-term survival objectives ahead of short-term earnings. Prochaska underlines, by means of statistics, that one in seventy-five American companies operates in the red, while in Japan it is one in five. Another Japanese belief is the equation of high quality with a successful new product, along with an opportunistic customer orientation for commercial success. While this seems obvious, the Japanese really believe in, and live by this principle. Since individual interests are aligned with and integrated into group and venture interests over the long term, there is not much personal risk or pressure to build up a solid knowledge base for eventual product and process innovation.

Gerstenfeld and Sumiyoshi (1980) take similar underlying elements but structure them in terms of consensus decision-making, lifetime employment, incentive, and promotion mechanisms. Associated with these mechanisms are a permanent job, group culture prioritizing company survival, quality products and services to satisfy customer demands and being externally opportunistic in this respect, along with daily learning and knowledge accumulation to create a solid knowledge base so as to reduce the probability of errors.

In the second phase of this booming period, Wood (1990) suggests that Japanese-style innovations have reversed conventional production management and links employee participation with innovations in production management, such as *kanban* and *kaizen*. Nonaka (1990) pushes the theorization on Japanese management and the innovation process further, looking at details beyond generic exogenous factors and the mere analytical aspects of innovation. For Nonaka, innovation is a product of the interaction between necessity and chance, order and disorder, continuity and discontinuity, as well as of difficulties in predicting or duplicating redundancy, chance, uncertainty, or even chaos. Focusing on redundant and overlapping organization and management, Nonaka reports multiple case examples, such as Fuji Xerox, Epson, and Canon, that exhibit redundancy in information, project teams, interdepartmental development processes, and interorganizational relations with suppliers – and redundancy of potential command. Promotion of mutual investigations and building trusting relationships are also part of such redundant and overlapping management to generate successful innovations.

On the other hand, Nonaka (1990) mentions several problems for innovation generation in Japanese firms (e.g., compromising in group thinking, high costs, and human exhaustion). The idea of needing information creation, and not only information flow and processing, in R&D activities is also reflected in Nonaka's framework (1988) of middle-up-down management, instead of the continuum between top-down and bottom-up. Using the Honda City example, Nonaka (1988) proposes a multilevel information creation process, synthesizing both deductive and inductive management. The idea of information redundancy and creation paved the way for Nonaka's later theorization of knowledge-creating organizations (Spender, 2013; Xu, 2013). Referring to the notion of "knowledge-creating organization" (Nonaka, 1990), Nonaka (1991) identifies the potential of innovation-creating new knowledge, instead of objective information processing, as the centerpiece of the Japanese management approach. Through a knowledge spiral, moving from metaphor to model, from chaos to concept, knowledge is created and converted from its tacit to its explicit type. Recognized as his major contribution to organizational theory, Nonaka's socialization-externalization-combination-internalization (SECI) model (Nonaka and Takeuchi, 1995) and the concept of *ba* (a shared context where knowledge is created; Nonaka and Konno, 1998) have also contributed to the field of strategy and technology and innovation management (Westney, 2020).

Some later scholarly works during this period, such as Mowery and Teece (1993) and Souder and Song (1998), often compare Japanese innovation with that of the United States. Mowery and Teece observe evidence of the end of postwar US technological hegemony and the rise of Japanese innovation. The comparative empirical work by Souder and Song suggests a reinforcement of the contingency management theory to consider the nature of the surrounding conditions in managing new product development (NPD). Unlike US NPD,

Japanese NPD is characterized by assigning high levels of technical expertise and assuring top management support and control as pivotal success factors.

Critiques of Traditionalism and Uniqueness

As illustrated earlier, Japanese management is shown as unique and different from that of the West, partly due to its traditions and culture rooted in its people, management and society. Looking at the essential differences between Japanese and Western management, Howard and Teramoto (1981) distinguish "meta-cultural" from cultural aspects. That is, Japanese people understand how decisions are made through their culture while Westerners do not, according to the authors. They introduce the concept of *nemawashi* as the "political" processes used to reach an understanding before any official decision-making procedures are initiated. The single word *nemawashi* contains all the meanings of the decision-making process, like "communication," "conflict," "control," "cooperation," "confrontation," "negotiation," and so on. This is what is argued as being the foundation for the creation of new social institutions in Japan during the postwar period, based on Japanese traditions, to improve industrial efficiency through improved decision-making that involves all stakeholders at different levels. In brief, Japanese decision-making methods have evolved to fit the specific context, though always in line with the nation's cultural tradition.

An early critique of Japanese management is that of Keys and Miller (1984), which identifies several competing theories explaining the impressive performance of Japanese businesses, correctly but only partially shedding light on the complexity of Japan's success and managerial achievement. The jungle of theories described by Keys and Miller includes examples like "just-in-time" in manufacturing management, quality control, the popular "Seven S" (i.e., superordinate goals, strategy, structure, systems, staff, skills, and style) theory (Pascale and Athos, 1981), organizational Theory Z (Ouchi, 1981), and human resources development (Hatvany and Pucik, 1981).To put this theory jungle in order, Keys and Miller identify common elements and models through mental factor analysis and recognize three underlying factors for a set of management practices: long-run planning horizon (e.g., articulation of company philosophy, growth of implicit control systems), commitment to lifetime employment (e.g., socialization process in hiring and integration, nonspecialized career paths), and collective responsibility (e.g., trust and interdependence, emphasis on teamwork and cooperation).

Similarly, Yang (1984) criticizes several Japanese management practices, echoing the concerns raised by Keys and Miller and underlining the double-edged effects of methods like *ringi* and the bottom-up decision-making process.

In practice, *ringi*-consensus management has subtle objectives and significance in Japan. While also being time-consuming (Drucker, 1971) Yang points out that the consensus-building process appeases factions in an organization rather than leading to better decisions. The issue seems to lie in whether the leadership can create a transparent communication culture in the organization and, consequently, participative management processes or it adheres to what Yang criticizes as *tatemae*-formality. Instead of a bottom-up or mid-up-down process (Nonaka, 1988), it is a handful of *jitsuryoku-sha* executives belonging to the mainstream faction led by the CEO that make important decisions. The decisions are made first, engaging in behind-the-scenes persuasion, before the formal *ringi* document is circulated for signatures. Consequently, potential disagreements to improve the decision quality are likely to come from executives within the *jitsuryoku-sha* group, as outsiders can make proposals but chances of acceptance are remote. Even if the bottom-up decision-making starts with proposals by lower-level managers, there is a tendency to propose what is believed to be the wishes of the superiors. Therefore, the bottom-up process merely disguises the true decision-making pattern, which generally runs from the top down. Sethi, Namiki, and Swanson (1984) also detect some early signs of the decline of the Japanese management system, as Japanese companies acquire American techniques to break away from their managerial traditions. In addition, younger Japanese employees, influenced by Western culture and nontraditional values, are less willing to make personal sacrifices (Yang, 1984). In sum, significant changes occurred in the Japanese business and management system, affecting core concepts and practices like lifetime employment, the seniority-based wage system, and consensus decision-making, which are regarded as the most distinctive and widely appreciated characteristics of Japanese management.

The earlier scholarly treatment of Japanese management often ignores the role of the environment (Nonaka and Johansson, 1985), although some soft factors, like lifetime employment, might be a result of the contingent development of the external environment (Kotabe, 2020). External factors that have contributed to internal changes in Japanese management traditions include the slowdown of Japanese economic growth, the rise of other low-cost providers from South Korea and Taiwan, and changes in the profile of Japan's younger generations. While most academics have attributed the occurrence of changes to external factors, Ornatowski (1998) also mentions the influence of shifts in international competitive positions, the structure of the Japanese economy, and employees' attitudes toward work. After a period of time when the United States learned Japanese management, hi-tech industries, like electronics, telecommunications, and biotechnology, were still largely influenced by Silicon

Valley management practices instead of deploying traditional Japanese management. Lifetime employment practices appeared to be troublesome, heavily affecting industries with excess capacity, like steel, shipbuilding, and aluminum. Indeed, in-house training related to lifetime employment made it difficult for companies to find adequate talent for the high-tech area and to develop new competitiveness due to the lack of the practice of seeking external talent. This talent and capability shortage was also tied to the seniority-based promotion and wage system, coupled with lifetime employment (Sethi et al., 1984).

Without denying the role of traditional Japanese management, Buckley and Mirza (1985) argue that other factors have also contributed to Japan's success: historical factors, investments in R&D (despite a complex relation with success), attention to detail and in particular to production techniques (Miyajima [1986] confirms the task-oriented organization ideology of Japanese managers), quality control and marketing (mostly originating from the United States), and a well-developed use of subcontractors to form an industrial ecosystem. Buckley and Mirza underline that Japan has a good reputation in cars, electrical goods, and microelectronics but is at a disadvantage in primary industries and services, like banking, insurance, shipping, mining, and foreign investment. In addition, the uniqueness of Japanese management, as separate from Western management, is questioned – and indeed the differences are smaller in the real world. Buckley and Mirza (1985) further distinguish and compare an ideal management set between the Westerner and Japan in terms of organizational principles, decision-making and communication, personnel system/labor management, and human relations and values. This argument essentially coincides with the discussions in Ouchi (1981) and Pascale and Athos (1981) around how to develop a superior management style, able to bring together the best of Japanese management and American management.

From Soft to Hard Factors

While most of the early discussions on Japanese management focus on "soft" elements (skill, staff, style, and superordinate goals), like the Seven S, Nonaka and Johansson (1985) emphasize the role of "hard" factors (strategy, structure, and system) in helping Japanese firms face the challenges of turbulent environments. Organizational learning in Japanese firms is brought to the fore, building the foundations of the knowledge school of management (i.e., Nonaka, 1991; Nonaka and Takeuchi, 1995), a major contribution to the area of strategy.

Besides the soft factors, Japanese companies are also experienced in the learning process to scan the environment for the needed task execution, as shown by the opportunistic behavior oriented to customers mentioned by

Gerstenfeld and Sumiyoshi (1980) and Prochaska (1980). In addition, corporate learning is shaped by corporate culture, stimulating information/knowledge sharing, consensus participation, and decision-making. Thus, organizations learn over time and continuously cope and interact with the environment. Through on-the-job training and the lifetime employment system, hard skills emerge in Japanese companies thanks to the extensive industrial experience acquired (Nonaka and Johansson, 1985). In the revisited Japanese management of Keys et al. (1994), learning is included to sequentially mediate among external forces, management practices, and organizational effectiveness. Indeed, Westney (2020) recognizes that Japanese management has contributed to the field of strategy as bridging the later-developed models on capabilities. Examples are the early works of Kagono et al. (1985) and Itami and Roehl (1987), which largely anticipate the capabilities perspective that is mainstream in strategy studies, although this is seldom recognized in the current strategy literature.

Convergences/Divergences and Controversies

In view of the preceding discussion, we can observe the emergence of a scholarly debate on whether Japanese management is uniquely differentiated from Western management (e.g., Buckley and Mirza, 1985), mainly meaning American management. Dunphy (1987) formalizes this debate by reviewing the historical evolution of Japanese organizations and management to describe convergences and divergences. Five periods of this conceptual evolution are identified: before 1970 – rise of the convergence theory; 1970–1973 – growing doubts about convergence with the West; 1974–1977 – strategic choice versus determinism; 1978–1980 – comparative studies of personnel practices; 1981–1983 – emergence of voluntarism. Each period in Dunphy's review is relatively short, but we can trace an evolution from the convergence view of Western scholars to the development of a divergent view of Japanese management as differing from Western management.

In fact, Dunphy summarizes this evolution process from an initial convergent view, not differentiating management in Japan and the West, to rising doubts on convergence in the early 1970s, to a focus on strategy and structure linked with cultural determinism in the mid-1970s and on personnel practices comparisons, reflecting on the assumptions of the divergent view in the late 1970s. At the same time, some results also suggest that internal labor management is a rational choice of managers interested in financial returns, not based on the repetition of traditional solutions (e.g., Levine and Kawada, 1980; Fruin, 1980). According to Dunphy, the early 1980s period recognized the uniqueness of

Japanese management, with data showing no decrease in Japanese management practices in previous decades (e.g., Ballon, 1983; Kubota, 1982; Takezawa and Whitehill, 1981). Meanwhile, other scholars argued for the convergence of both Japanese and Western management into a mixed model (e.g., Ouchi, 1981; Pascale and Athos, 1981). Therefore, in Dunphy's opinion, the uniqueness of Japanese management practices may be a voluntary choice by elites or managers to mindfully respond to the particular economic and cultural environment.

Mroczkowski and Hanaoka (1989) continue along this line of voluntarism thinking in the sense that they regard management changes in Japan as adaptations to the external markets and environments along a trajectory from being a low-cost imitator to an exporter (in order to stimulate the domestic economy) to competing in the upper markets with quality and innovation (partly due to appreciation of the yen). Such strategic changes also require transformations and shifts in employment relations, referring to the inherent weaknesses of Japanese management. In fact, lifetime commitment and groupism encourage employee dependency and suppress individual creativity, a seniority-based system creates gridlock for middle managers and younger talents, while employment discrimination penalizes nonlifelong employees and prevents a free horizontal labor market from developing (Odaka, 1986).

The decreased economic growth rate in the 1970s demanded more flexibility in the employment and reward system (Mroczkowski and Hanaoka, 1989). The appreciation of the dollar in the early 1980s postponed labor pressure, but the later rise of the yen's value in 1985 required cost control and innovation to retain competitiveness and face three main challenges: remaining cost competitive without resorting to massive layoffs, continuing to motivate employees and managers in the new environment and redesigning employment relationships to take advantage of the old system while fostering creativity. Hence, Mroczkowski and Hanaoka describe the emergence of a new management paradigm featuring a restructuring of employment methods and wage control, a new motivational system based on performance evaluation and rewards – changing the importance of seniority, merging performance appraisal and merit rating with Japanese style management – and a redesign of employment relationships relying on a multitrack employment system. The 1980s' booming scholarly interest in Japanese management, with heated debates and profound contributions to management theory, ended with the transformation of Japanese management for the sake of continuing to innovate its management theory and practices for further success.

In a later review, Sullivan (1992) interprets earlier works on Japanese management as spotlights on different parts of a complex body of Japanese management theory, with both positive and negative elements. Introducing the *nihonjiron* ideologies, which created a legitimizing basis for Japan's economic and business life, but also questioning their applicability in businessmen's actions, Sullivan suggests that Japan's elegant management philosophies may not actually reflect reality. For instance, Ouchi's Theory Z might be a nice justification for Japanese companies to expose in front of their Western counterparts; however, echoes of *tatemae* (Yang, 1984) do remain. The causes and consequences of this convergence and divergence are fused in reality, determined by the voluntary decisions of scholars and managers. Robinson and Schroeder (1993) show that some typical Japanese management practices can indeed be traced back to their American origins, like the Training Within Industry (TWI) program introduced into Japan by the United States in 1949. The development of *kaizen* (continuous improvement), the Toyota Production System (the first just-in-time system), and progressive human relations may actually have been influenced by TWI. Warner (1994) also claims that the imported Taylorism was an important factor in the establishment of Total Quality Management (TQM) in Japan and the contribution of Japanese management was to absorb and adapt such imported concepts and practices to an organization-oriented context.

Enduring Interests in Japanese Management Research

Managerial interest in Japanese management in the West fell drastically in the mid-1990s, as the Japanese recession seemed to last long with hardly any sign of recovery, but academic interest endured (Endo et al., 2015; Makino and Lehmberg, 2020; Westney, 2020). Our WoS search results also show a stable academic output in Japanese management journal publications, despite a decline in comparison with the booming period of the 1980s.

Ornatowski (1998) suggests it is about the evolution of Japanese style of human resources management rather than reaching its end, referring to the substitutive forms of the seniority-based wage system (*nenko*), promotion, and lifetime employment. Large corporations placed more emphasis on innovation in products, marketing, and services, while manufacturers relocated their production bases overseas to deal with high labor costs and, at the same time, implemented performance-based pay and promotion systems in Japan. Japanese companies aimed at new human resources management practices for corporate organizational restructuring to respond to strategy diversification (Steffensen, 1998). The challenges not only had to do with what Ornatowski (1998) says about internationalization, technological changes, economic recession, and social changes, but also involved the paradigmatic breakthroughs within digital info-communication technologies and new types of global networks, industrialization, and corporate alliances. Steffensen (1998, p. 516) highlights the network quality of Japanese industrial organizations, with efficient supply chain management, flexible production designs, organizational learning, and strenuous R&D activities. Japan's characteristic multilateral interfirm networks, like *keiretsu*, feature long-term internalized transactions and cross-industry cooperation. This prevailing Japanese style of interorganizational structures is strongly based on human networks and social exchange dynamics. Family roots are also emphasized as the institutional logic and source of Japanese corporate networks and management practices (Bhappu, 2000).

The collapse of Japan's bubble economy in the early 1990s and ensuing sluggish performance of many of its MNEs turned the secrets of the Japanese management system into shackles, preventing future growth (Kishi, 2003). Since the late 1990s, changes have been implemented in governance mechanisms, corporate structures, labor relations and employment practices (Collinson and Rugman, 2008). The rise of the Chinese economy has also greatly influenced the transformation of Japanese management practices (Horn and Cross, 2009).

Studies with a laudatory tone on the crucial influence of Japanese management have essentially disappeared in the twenty-first century, with mainstream research concentrating on the inherent problems of Japanese management (Hasegawa, 2006). For instance, Warner (2011) criticizes Japanese management given its economic performance, stating that it is losing its position as the "flavor of the month." The three pillars of Japanese management (seniority system, lifetime employment, and company union) seem no longer viable, while Japan's legendary reputation for product quality appears greatly diminished. According to Warner (2011), not many new concepts or practices are offered in terms of management innovation in comparison with past contributions, such as the adaptation and refinement of Taylorism in the Japanese context (just-in-time, total quality management, and zero defects).

Nonetheless, some recent studies have reexamined the adjustments and transformations of Japanese management. For example, Fitzgerald and Rowley (2015) underline the changes adopted by Japanese MNEs to enhance their competitiveness, among which are shifting from production to buyer-driven global value chains, cross-border vertical specialization, global factory strategies, and strategic alliances and competitive relationships. The review by Adler and Hiromoto (2012) on Kyocera's Amoeba system illustrates a distinctive entrepreneurial culture with an ability to multiply and change shape in response to the environment. Furusawa, Brewster, and Takashina (2016) empirically test the transnationality of Japanese MNEs in international human resources management and find that social capital and geocentric staffing mediate the relationship between normative or system integration and transnationality.

3 The Invisible Part of the Iceberg: Further Thoughts on Japanese Management

According to Hirotaka Takeuchi, one of the reasons why Japanese businesses are good at surviving crises is their dedication to responding to the needs of people first, namely employees and the community, before dealing with other priorities, with the moral purpose of serving the common good (Gerdeman, 2020). The review of Japanese management in Section 2 provided an overview of the scholarly works published in quality academic journals in English over the period 1961–2021. We recognize that the review process was selective and omissions may have occurred, but we trust that it reflects the evolution and different dimensions of the whole elephant drawn in the field of Japanese management. The comprehensive integration of Western and Japanese academic sources from WoS yielded an in-depth analysis of Japanese management facts, including its sources, evolution, and controversies – though disagreement may remain. As Mroczkowski and Hanaoka (1989) point out, most of the earlier books and articles on Japanese management published in the West were written by non-Japanese observers, often with the aim of criticizing the failures of Western management, which created the myth of Japanese management. In this section, we intend to provide an insider's view of Japanese management from Japan. Some of the views expressed here may echo certain literature discussed earlier based on similar foundations.

Japanese-Style Management and Economic Growth

The evolution of Japanese-style management is tightly linked to the economic development of Japan (Nonaka and Johansson, 1985; Kotabe, 2020). For example, lifetime employment was the product of a specific historical context in which skilled labor was in short supply during the years after World War II. Later, the seniority-based system became dysfunctional when the external competitive environment started to demand creativity, especially after the 1990s, when digitalization took place in the global business environment. Endo et al. (2015) highlight the relevance of contextual factors for examining Japanese firms. As well, Okubayashi (1995) embedded the discussion of Japanese management within a dynamic context and extensive descriptions, for example the establishment of traditional Japanese management along with the role of government toward the business world and the recovery of employers' associations during the rapid economic growth era. Table 1 summarizes the

Table 1 Relationships between Japanese management and economic development in the Japanese economic growth period

Period	Relationships between Japanese management and economic development
Latter half 1950s – First half 1960s	Economic growth → Japanese-style management
Latter half 1960s – Early 1970s	Japanese-style management ←→ Economic growth
Mid 1970s – First half 1980s	Japanese-style management → Economic growth

relationship between Japanese-style management and economic development over time, showing a bidirectional, cause-and-effect link depending on the period of economic growth. We would first like to distinguish three types of Japanese enterprises, before delving further into the discussion of Japanese management.

Types of Japanese Managers and Enterprises

Different stakeholders contributed to the rapid and stable economic growth of post-WWII Japan. Yoshino (1968) observes three factors giving rise to a new phase of business leadership and consequently contributing to economic recovery and development. First, economic reforms dissolved the entrenched Zaibatsu system, leading to the popularization of corporate ownership; second, post-war occupation gave young upper-middle managers the chance to emerge as outstanding top executives, with entrepreneurial spirit and new ideas in contrast to the Zaibatsu's conservative characteristics; third, a number of very successful founder-type entrepreneurs seized the opportunity to exert brilliant leadership. Some examples of the latter are Konosuke Matsushita of Matsushita Electric, Masaru Ibuka of Sony, Soichiro Honda of Honda Motors, and Shojiro Ishibashi of Bridgestone Tires. The former may be exemplified by Chikara Kurata of Hitachi and Taizo Ishizaka of Toshiba. A study by Aonuma (1965) highlights that only ninety out of 1,500 top executives (6 percent) in top-ranking large enterprises held their position through ownership in 1962, among which thirty were the founders. Conversely, the percentage of owner-managers was 80 percent in 1900 and almost 50 percent in 1925.

The post-war data show clear separation of management from ownership and progress toward professionalization of management in Japan (Yoshino, 1968). We may call the managers who also have ownership of corporations owner-managers

Table 2 Types of Japanese enterprises

Type	Name	Size	Ownership vs. Leadership	Management Style
A	Large Managerial Enterprises	Large	Separated	Professional Management
B	Large Capitalistic Enterprises	Large	Combined	Owner-Management / Entrepreneurship
C	Small and Medium-Sized Capitalistic Enterprises	Small and Medium	Combined	Owner-Management / Entrepreneurship

and entrepreneur/founder-managers, different from professional managers, namely hired, salaried managers. Extending the discussion of managers to enterprises, we can distinguish three types of enterprises: (a) large managerial enterprises, (b) large capitalist enterprises, and (c) small and medium-sized enterprises (SMEs) as capitalist enterprises (Kikkawa, 2014) (see Table 2). Seldom are SMEs also managerial enterprises, able to give professional managers a larger amount of power. Consequently, the managers who shaped Japan's new business ideology were mainly those in large managerial enterprises, where professional managers exerted more real power than the owners, in comparison with capitalist enterprises led by managers with ownership. Yoshino (1968) illustrates this by discussing the emergence of managerial ideology in post-war Japan, along with the empirical data provided by Aonuma (1965), described earlier.

Sugimoto and Mouer (1982) criticize the tendency to regard Japan as a homogeneous country and, indeed, the management style and dominant logic of the three types of enterprises present in Japan are different, even though they are all Japanese enterprises. As Yoshino (1968: 95) explicitly points out, "business ideology is not monolithic"; rather, it is continually evolving, shaped and revised by managers. Before Japan's economic bubble burst, if one had asked the question "To whom does a company belong?", the answer would have clearly been "the employees" in case (a) and "the owners" in case (c). As for (b), some might have answered "the employees" and others "the owners." In a capitalistic country, the ownership of a company should, by definition, be in the hands of its shareholders-owners. Yet, the situation is less clear in the

Japanese context, where in large managerial enterprises it is considered natural to think that "the company belongs to the employees." This is unique to Japanese management operated in a typical Japanese style. In fact, it is often said that, even in Japan, Japanese-style management was just a partial phenomenon, detectable in particular types of enterprises, and it did not become prevalent throughout the nation. From an insider's point of view, it is necessary to clarify that not all Japanese enterprises ran their business by following Japanese-style management even when it was praised. It was mostly those led by professional managers that developed a unique management style, soon to be known internationally as "Japanese-style management" (Kikkawa, 2004).

Nonetheless, SMEs have also played an important role in contributing to economic growth, although this is not emphasized in Japanese business history in general. Starting around World War I, when Japan attained an internationally higher level of economic growth, the issue of the dual structure of the economy came to the fore. In this dual structure, SMEs and the distribution sector were regarded as symbols of vulnerability, whereas large enterprises were placed at the opposite end of the spectrum, since they had strength. The post-WWI wage differentials by company size were often referred to as an example of the vulnerability of SMEs. The average wage by company size was then equalized, due to the sharp decline in real wages that occurred right after Japan's defeat in WWII, but the wage differentials emerged again in the 1950s. The ubiquitous presence of significant wage disparities between large enterprises and SMEs also created opportunities for Japanese large manufacturers to extensively utilize subsidiaries (no consolidated financial statements were required by law), affiliated firms, and hierarchical subcontractors at different levels in the labor-intensive portion of the supply chain (Yoshino, 1968) to form the business ecosystem. Thus, SMEs constituted an important part of the sizeable business ecosystems led by large enterprises, contributing their abilities, skills, and knowledge to fuel national innovation.

Professional Managers and Japanese-style Management

Large managerial enterprises were only a minority in Japan before World War II, as Aonuma (1965) demonstrated, and only a small amount of professional managers existed. Although these hired executives played an important role in the pre-war Zaibatsu, they often "had to work under the strict rules as well as under the general direction of the family" (Yoshino, 1968). Nevertheless, professional managers and managerial enterprises had become the norm by the mid-1950s, characterized by rapid economic growth. While the first post-war phase had been crisis-ridden, the second phase was one of recovery and rapid growth, the time when the managerial ideology was articulated, whereas in the third phase, the early 1960s, business leaders became self-critical and went in search of a new ideology (Yoshino, 1968). Around that time, the answer to the question "To whom does a company belong?" in Japan's large enterprises mostly came to be "the employees." Top management was also regarded as belonging to the category of employees, albeit the most successful employees.

Even in large capitalist enterprises, such as Toyota Motor, Panasonic, Idemitsu Kosan, Suntory, Ajinomoto, Bridgestone, Canon, Sanyo Electric, Sharp, Sony, and Honda Motor, professional managers represented a growing portion of the top management as company size grew. The idea that "A company belongs to all its employees" increasingly took hold, creating a mixed situation in large capitalistic firms in terms of "ownership" conceptualization. The idea that the employees are the owners of the business spread across large enterprises, both managerial and capitalistic. Regardless of company type, decision-making to maximize benefits to the employees was supported by a sense of unity between labor and management. This distinctive management approach was established in large enterprises at the end of Japan's rapid economic growth period, when the term "Japanese-style management" or "Japanese management" came to be popularized.

Differently from the Soviet Union's "belonging to the workers" ideology, Japan's concept of "belonging to the employees" includes top managers, who are also salarymen, and entails a long-term view of property "ownership," unlike American enterprises, which rely on shareholder ownership (Kikkawa, 2014). The second post-war phase of the Japanese economy was marked by great enthusiasm in accepting the "American managerial ideology, concepts and techniques," as optimism flourished in the economy and business elites grew more aware of social responsibility beyond the business environment (Yoshino, 1968: 97). Japanese managerial ideology developments, such as the Doyukai declaration of 1956, were considered a fusion of modern American business philosophy and traditional Japanese business mentality (Tsuchiya, 1960). The unprecedented growth opportunities of the late 1950s and early 1960s drove Japanese enterprises to expand continuously and diversify (Yoshino, 1968), so much so that Kikkawa (1995a) argues that the dominant logic of Japan's managerial enterprises was their growth-oriented decision-making, contributing to Japan's relatively strong economic growth after WWII right until the mid 1980s.

The excessive capacity and intense competition caused by their expansive strategies worsened the performance of poorly managed leading firms, while thoughtful business leaders looked for solutions to new challenges. That is when the Doyukai's Kansai Chapter released "Managerial Ideology in a New

Environment" in 1964 (Yoshino, 1968), which featured five proposals discussing the keystones of Japanese management. On the one hand, the first proposal of the declaration recognized the need to pursue profit in the management of private enterprises, in contrast with the prewar disregard for the matter. On the other hand, the other four proposals were not related to profitability but concerned the individual workers and their creativity, fair competition and climate, responsibilities to the local community, and direct and indirect responsibilities to the whole of society.

People Management

As the literature review in Section 2 shows, three items, namely lifetime employment, the seniority-based system, and an enterprise union (Warner, 2011), are frequently referred to as the three pillars or three sacred treasures of Japanese-style management (Okubayashi, 1995). All three items correspond to the organizational employment system (Jacoby, 2005) and involve people management or labor relations, a subsystem located at the core of Japanese management. In this sense, Kikkawa (2014: 283) also defines Japanese-style management as the "management which seeks to maximize the benefits of employees, based on harmonious labor-management relations."

As stated in the Doyukai declaration of 1964, Japanese management integrates profitability and social responsibility into managerial principles and activities, a concept echoed by Takeuchi's reasoning on how Japanese businesses manage to survive and withstand crises, namely by serving the common good (Gerdeman, 2020). This social responsibility is broadly defined across multiple levels: individual, firm, community, industry, and society. Sakikawa (2012) praises the attitude and behavior of Japanese people during the triple disaster (i.e., massive earthquake, tsunami, and nuclear accident) experienced by the country in 2011, mentioning their preparedness, discipline, and teamwork. Resilience, coordination, altruism, perseverance, and other traditional Japanese qualities are regarded as equally crucial in helping companies and the economy as a whole survive and overcome disasters and crises.

This human side of Japanese management is not only a unique aspect but also a main factor in sustaining performance. Business historians place the formulation of Japanese-style people management relations in the postwar period of relatively high economic growth, when Japan's workers at production sites became actively involved in efficient production and strict quality control (Kikkawa, 2014). When Udagawa et al. (1995) examine the introduction of quality control in Japan and discuss the formulation of the Japanese-style production system, they attach great importance to changes in competitive conditions in the first half of the 1960s, arguing that Total Quality Control (TQC) or Quality Control (QC) circles were introduced against a background of management crisis or heightened sense of crisis caused by such changes. Incidentally, TQC means quality control activities in which all workers participate and QC circles are small groups that conduct quality control activities at worksites. After World War II, Japanese enterprises imported various management methods from the United States (see, for instance, Robinson and Schroeder, 1993; Warner, 1994). However, most of them did not take root as they were but assumed Japanized forms. A typical example may be doing QC using statistical methods imported from the United States, which took root in Japanese enterprises after being transformed into the TQC or QC circles.

Discussions on how Japanese enterprises do Quality Control are based on case studies of Komatsu, Panasonic, Toyota Motor, Nissan Motor, and other companies. The previously mentioned changes in competitive conditions in the first half of the 1960s refer to situations like the liberalization of trade and capital for Komatsu, the maturation of its domestic market for Panasonic, the defeat in the first BC War (Bluebird vs. Corona war) for Toyota Motor, the defeat in the second BC War for Nissan Motor, and so on. In short, Udagawa et al. (1995) suggest that reacting to a crisis actually benefitted some major Japanese enterprises at that time, which resulted in the formulation of both Japanese-style people management and the Japanese-style production system. As described, therefore, Japanese-style people/labor management relations, or Japanese management, are widely believed by scholars of Japanese labor history to have been established in the early 1960s. Jacoby (2012) even asserts that High-Performance Work Practices (HPWP), a strategic human resources management mechanism popular in the West, came from the HRM side of the Toyota Production System.

Japanese-Style Management and Innovation

Though nonmarket competition tended to resist the introduction of new technologies, Japan's large managerial enterprises, which regarded themselves as "belonging to the employees," were free from those factors that prevented enterprises in the United States and the Soviet Union from introducing new technologies and pursuing business growth (Kikkawa, 2014). The tradition of learning from foreign technology may be traced back to Dutch Learning in the Edo era (1603–1867), by which samurai intellectuals gained knowledge of Western technology. Although companies appeared in Japan during the Meiji era (1868–1912) in the modern context and Okubayashi (1995) considers that some elements of traditional Japanese management started their development in the industrialization process during this period (after World War I), market economy was significantly developed during the Edo period with the "Three Great Merchant Houses" in Kyoto, Osaka, and Edo (Miyamoto, 1996; 2007). It is especially relevant from a historian's perspective as a breakthrough innovation for its newness of business innovation in a Japan isolated from the rest of the world at that time, when a market economy was developed in a still-feudal society. The massive learning from foreigners was repeated in the postwar era, when Japanese industries were eager to import technologies from abroad to make the country one of the leading industrial nations. In the period 1950–1966, 60 percent of technology license contracts were with American firms (Yoshino, 1968). That eventually resulted in the Japanese-style management based on the collaborative labor-management relations aimed at maximizing employee profits with incremental technological innovations to cumulatively and continuously improve (*kaizen*) technology and production. Although breakthrough innovation (e.g., the discovery of the umami taste by Ajinomoto) also occurred during this period of high growth (i.e., the Japanese economy grew at an average annual rate of 10.4 percent from 1956 to 1970) and, later on, stable economic development in Japan until the 1980s (i.e., albeit at a lower economic growth rate, Japanese development still was higher than that of other developed Western countries) (Kikkawa, 2007), the *kaizen* type of incremental innovations seemed to be dominating.

As Table 1 addresses, Japanese economic growth and Japanese management interacted during this period. The continuous expanding domestic market and demands sustained a long-term relatively high economic growth, which in turn required Japanese corporations to constantly enhance their organizational capabilities, fueled by innovative entrepreneurial activities. The three pillars of Japanese management constitute an organization-oriented employment system (Jacoby, 2005), which fosters firm-specific knowledge, skills, and capabilities through the recruitment of new college graduates and guaranteed employment for the creation of tacit knowledge flows, in contrast to explicit knowledge (Nonaka, Toyama, and Hirata, 2008). Tacit knowledge is essential for Japanese organizations to preserve their unique competitiveness and ensure that their people and embedded knowledge are valuable, rare, and inimitable but, at the same time, organizable, so as to obtain economic returns. Similarly, Ray and Little (2001) stress the importance of the collective tacit knowledge and practices of Japanese workplaces (*ba*) for "friction-free" communication and knowledge generation. In this sense, lifetime employment not only contributes to the development of firm-specific skills and tacit knowledge, but also earns the loyalty of employees in exchange for job security. Meanwhile, the seniority system does not work in isolation but is tied to lifetime employment (Sakikawa, 2012). That is, because of lifetime employment, the seniority system is utilized; given that employees are evaluated based on tenure or seniority, lifetime employment is viable and effective. As the internal labor market is well developed, the external labor market's development is limited.

Arguably, Japanese-style people management was suitable for creating incremental technological innovation – which is generated gradually, cumulatively, and continuously, in contrast with radical technological innovation – at production sites. Even the breakthrough innovative discovery of Ajinomoto could be considered as a cumulation of in-company incremental innovations. Postwar Japanese enterprises achieved great success in the development of applied technologies, owing to an ecosystem including their in-company or intracompany systems and intercompany systems (Kikkawa, 1995b). In this regard, Okubayashi (1995) also reflects the new characteristics of Japanese management beyond the "Three Sacred Pillars" in the stable economic growth period in these two systems. Concerning the intracompany systems, the redundant and overlapping organization and management was favorable for Japanese innovation (Nonaka, 1990). In promoting technological development, valuable management practices were introduced, such as setting business objectives from a long-term perspective, horizontal and flexible organizational structure and employment practices like long-term employment, internal transfer, and internal promotion systems (Kikkawa, 1995b). A flat organization equipped with IT in an open-space big office where managers and clerks work together was also a new trend of office organization (Okubayashi, 1995).

Long-term business objectives enabled investments in technological development with no expectation of producing immediate effects, in addition to empowering the continuity and stability of Research and Development (R&D). A horizontal and flexible organizational structure facilitated "horizontal" intracompany information and knowledge flows. Thanks to job rotation, multitasked lifetime employees and teams maintained close communication across divisions within the company, such as research, design, manufacturing, and sales, and allowed the free flow of necessary information, skills, and knowledge. Long-term employment and the internal promotion system lowered resistance to the introduction of new technologies, which often caused problems in Western countries. Also, additional incentives were put in place for both labor and management to conduct in-house education and training, especially centered around on-the-job (OJT) training, namely activities carried out in the workplace during working hours to become familiar with the working environment.

As for the intercompany systems, it was important to have long-term transactional relationships among Japanese enterprises. In such relationships goods, information, and knowledge are exchanged, shared, and transferred, with a collaborative approach adopted by all parties in the network and business ecosystem. This enterprise group resembles the Zaibatsu but differs because it is not controlled by a holding company. With a loose network of membership companies, these continuous intercompany relationships involve many aspects to create cohesion, maintained by "interlocking shareholding," "Keiretsu financing," or "interlocking Directorates" (Okubayashai, 1995). Japanese enterprises are good at sensing, learning and channeling relevant information and knowledge about customer demands so as to advance product development in a timely manner by accurately responding to them. This dynamic capability (Teece, 2007) enables Japanese enterprises to adjust their management and products within their ecosystem. The continuous sharing of knowledge in a long-term business relationship between suppliers and manufacturers also leads to frequent performance improvements in terms of production technology and efficiency.

It has been observed that this holds true not only for technology innovation but also for product, process, business model, and organizational innovation, as reflected in the Doyukai's 1964 pronouncement, which emphasized obtaining profit through the innovative and creative functions of management, namely "through technological innovations, market development, rationalization of business practices, and higher productivity" (Yoshino, 1968: 109). In addition, the pronouncement already promoted some of the current academic debate on the issue of sustainability in the field of management: that is, the pursuit of profit is not incompatible with social responsibility, and the fair pursuit of profit and its equitable distribution among stakeholders do contribute to economic growth, stability, and sustainability (Yoshino, 1968).

New Type of Japanese-Style Management

Academic interest endured albeit the stagnation and deterioration of Japan's economic development by the end of the twentieth century (Makino and Lehmberg, 2020; Westney, 2020), a phase in which Japanese enterprises began to face the challenge of maintaining their success in a highly competitive global business environment. The country's large enterprises have devoted a great deal of effort to solving this puzzle and reviving their past glories in the international arena. Rebuilding or renewing Japanese-style management to release the potential of the nation's talents is a crucial matter in this regard.

Challenges: Performance Deterioration and Management Dysfunction

Since the Plaza Accord of 1985, the performance and evaluation of Japanese enterprises have drastically deteriorated. In the mid 1980s, a positive opinion of Japan's enterprise systems was still dominant, reflecting the good performance of its economy. However, when the economic bubble burst at the beginning of the 1990s and the "lost decade" began, criticism of Japan's enterprise systems grew. Though the causes of such deterioration in performance were various, including a maturing domestic economy, recession, and global economic conditions, the criticism mainly targeted Japanese-style management, viewed as ineffective or dysfunctional (Frikola, 2006). Why was the type of management that had supported the "success" of the Japanese economy until the 1980s suddenly identified as the main cause of its "failure" in the 1990s? It seemed that traditional Japanese management would be forced to reflect and change.

Actually, after the burst of the economic bubble, Japanese-style management resulted in dysfunction. Its devitalization was triggered by the fact that large managerial enterprises lost their self-confidence and started to bring "shareholder-oriented management" to the fore, in contrast to the emergence of the stakeholder theory in the United States. In addition, industrial companies were required to raise money in the capital market due to the expansion of capital markets in Japan and the globalization of the financial sector, which accelerated in the latter half of the 1980s. To provide an example, it was not at all wrong for the once "employees-are-owners" large managerial enterprises to place importance on shareholders after the 1990s. Nonetheless, due to their loss of self-confidence and their regarding shareholder-oriented management as equivalent to the pursuit of short-term profits by the managers of such enterprises, a long-term vision was mostly absent. Sakikawa (2019) summarizes the differences in Japanese management during the postwar era and after the bubble burst by stating that the former was organic and coordinated, while the latter was market-oriented and competitive. This is reflected in multiple dimensions, like mutual benefits versus calculative exchanges for what concerns employment relations, trust-based corporate culture versus contract-based professional standards in terms of administrative rules, employment security versus profitability maximization with regard to priority, and trust-based long-term linkages versus market transactions based on short-term principles as for supply chain relations, among others.

For the purpose of raising funds in the capital market, Japan's large managerial enterprises transitioned to the American model of corporate management, which placed greater emphasis on financial measures, such as Return on Assets (ROA) and Return on Equity (ROE). While American enterprises enjoyed the "New Economy" in the 1990s, they also made aggressive investments as part of their strategies for achieving higher ROA or ROE through increased returns. By contrast, most of Japan's large managerial enterprises inhibited investments and tried to drive up their ratio of ROA and ROE by decreasing assets and equity (Kikkawa, 2005). As already pointed out by Hayashi (1978a), Japanese firms that develop into competitive multinationals are largely dependent upon managerial creativity for shaping effective means of control other than ownership and profits, in forms other than dividends. However, after the bubble burst, the risk-averse Japanese firms worked negatively, falling prey to the so-called "Inhibitory Mechanism of Investment." The top managers of large managerial enterprises were fearful and unable to make sufficient investments as part of the specific duty of their businesses, while the regular employees aggressively cooperated for the survival of their companies by inhibiting investments (Kikkawa, 2005). Somehow, this is also reflected in what Sullivan (1992) describes as "Theory F" (for fear), "to the point of avoiding decision which might lead to an error" (p. 82). As a result, the advantages of Japanese-style management, a long-term view and appropriate investment strategy, ceased to exist.

When looking back at Japan's business history, we can identify the occurrence of a major crisis whenever a change came about in relation to the global market. For example, the end of the Edo period was when Japanese society first encountered global capitalism upon the opening of ports resulting from the arrival of the Black Ships. The 1960s was when trade liberalization and capital liberalization began, also known as "the second arrival of the Black Ships." The trigger for the deterioration of Japan's economy from the "phase of success" to the "phase of failure" was the rapid appreciation of the yen following the Plaza Accord of 1985. When the Japanese market came to a standstill, Japanese enterprises had to find a way out by fighting a global "two-front war," namely pushing simultaneously into the expanding low-end market and the lucrative high-end market. Yet, the country's large managerial enterprises, which had lost their long-term perspective, still failed to make the necessary investments to engage in the "two-front war." What the Japanese economy and enterprises faced in the 1990s, the so-called "lost decade," was a partial crisis in the financial system, while the production system remained healthy. However, by mistaking this partial crisis for an overall crisis, Japanese enterprises lost their confidence. They mixed up shareholder-oriented management with the pursuit of short-term profits and set aside their long-term perspective, a key advantage of Japanese-style management. Based on research by Pudelko (2009), Warner (2011) wonders whether this is the end for Japanese-style management. Besides other general factors, Warner (2011) is particularly interested in comparing the Japanese situation with that of the fast-growing, catching-up Chinese enterprises, as well as those of other BRIC countries.

Rebuilding Japanese-Style Management

Not only do Western scholars call for changes in Japanese management (e.g., Horn and Cross, 2009; Warner, 2011), but also Japanese managers and scholars are aware of this essential need (e.g. Mroczkowski and Hanaoka, 1989; Sakikawa, 2012; Hirasaka, Kusaka, and Brogan, 2021). Japanese executives had believed that the disadvantages of the business environment would be outweighed by the strengths of the nation's enterprises. Nonetheless, following the rise of the yen in 1985, many companies realized that they were unable to fully maintain the "old system" and began to search for a new Japanese management system (Mroczkowski and Hanaoka, 1989).

It is worth noting here that the reality of history is often dynamic and evolving, namely a continuous process (Yoshino, 1968), while researchers tend to take a static snapshot in order to capture its essence for various investigation purposes. Japanese management theorization is no exception. In this regard, Horn and Cross (2009) recognize that certain misconceptions, oversimplifications, and misunderstandings about the realities of Japanese management are still widespread, especially in the Western literature. The currency appreciation made it very difficult for Japanese companies to keep their past rate of capital productivity, while their growth rate had already leveled off in the 1980s (Watanabe, 1987). Yet, they did react to changes in their environment. The Romu Gyosei Kenkyujo, a private research foundation, surveyed 1,900 Japanese companies and found that the ability/merit factor contributed 42.1 percent to pay raises against the seniority factor in 1978, which increased to 54 percent in 1987 (Mroczkowski and Hanaoka, 1989). Along with the seniority system, lifetime employment also was transformed, since it interfered with offering top talents high salaries. Labor mobility rose and the trend was expected to continue, with 75 percent of the surveyed businesses showing interest in a headhunter's offer (Watanabe, 1987; Mroczkowski and Hanaoka, 1989).

In spite of growing awareness of problems and changes underway, the burst of the economic bubble worsened the situation and encouraged further reforms. In the opinion of business historians, the dominant logic of management shifted, as Sakikawa (2019) suggests. The conflicting medium- and long-term interests of different stakeholders – in this specific case, shareholders and employees – took center stage, so that rebuilding Japanese-style management on new premises integrating both became paramount. The rebuilding was a transformation process to innovate the old system, aimed at hybridizing the commitment of long-term employment with merit-oriented people management, rather than the seniority system (Kikkawa, 2014). This new form needed to maintain long-term employment to ensure a sense of security among workers. On the other hand, it had to force through reforms, such as introducing a merit system by carrying out a thorough review of the seniority system, to motivate knowledge workers and especially the young generations.

After the 1990s, Japanese enterprises have had to fight difficult battles and face the two-pronged attack of breakthrough innovation in developed countries and disruptive innovation in emerging economies. They have kept growing by relying on incremental innovation targeting the "fertile Japanese market" and have built international competitiveness. However, this mechanism is losing effectiveness due to two factors. The first is that the Japanese market itself has scaled down, as a result of the country's depopulating society, and is no longer a "womb to nurture growth." The other factor is that the notion of national borders dividing markets by country is losing meaning because of how digitalization and technology have transformed global business, with the emergence of breakthrough disruptive innovation (Kikkawa, 2019).

In the latter context, Hirasaka et al. (2021) suggest a paradigmatic shift in management style and the adoption of a hybrid approach to create a new model, integrating both Western and Japanese ways of thinking and methods. Japanese firms have been among those investing the most in R&D, but their investments have failed to be translated into performance (Shikata, Goto, and Gemba, 2019). In examining comparative cases, such as Fujifilm versus Kodak and Nissan versus Sharp, Hirasaka et al. (2021) conclude that these Japanese companies differ in their corporate management arising from corporate culture, attitudes to external environmental changes, reactions to management crises, measures for structural reforms, commitment to innovation by top management, and so on.

In fast-changing and rapidly evolving environments, dynamism is induced by multiple dimensions, including technology, emerging markets' competition, and unpredictable crises, like COVID-19, and the degree of dynamism goes up owing to multiple sources and interactive effects (Zhang-Zhang, Rohlfer, and Varma, 2022). Faced with today's complex VUCA context, it is vital for Japanese enterprises to focus on and develop their core capabilities, reclaim their long-term people centric management, while supporting high performance through competitiveness. Successful examples are humanized cell production in Canon and Sony (Sakikawa, 2012), Amoeba management in Kyocera (Adler and Hiromoto, 2012; Kase, Choi, and Nonaka, 2022) or ambidextrous organizational capability in Fujifilm (Shibata et al., 2019). If this is achieved, then there will be a reemergence of the advantages of Japanese-style management, emphasizing the common good, surviving disruptive innovation, and sustaining competitive advantages. As Yoshino (1968) states, since the innovative process of the Japanese management system evolves over time, Japanese-style management can and must transform itself into a new management style, attaching importance to long-term employment but not to the seniority system.

4 Japanese Managers, Enterprises, and Industries: Some Insiders' View

Sections 2 and 3 discussed the general understanding of Japanese-style management, from both the Japanese and international perspectives. In spite of its ups and downs, we observe at its core a people centric view of the firm, which may be key to its long-time survival and sustainable development. Whether reflected in the three pillars or in a knowledge management perspective for innovation, Japanese management and practices are in essence people-based and aim to cultivate individual capabilities and knowledge so as to contribute to firm growth. This is not only about employment relations, human resources management, or labor management, but it entails a broader approach to strategically manage people within and around the organization, namely all stakeholders in the business ecosystem, for the purpose of knowledge capture, absorption, transfer, and creation. Such a people centric view of the firm may be based on the knowledge-worker perspective in the knowledge school of management for sustainable performance (Zhang-Zhang, Rohlfer, and Varma, 2022). Creativity, technology, innovation, and knowledge have been highlighted as relevant for management, industrial development, and economic growth (Yoshino, 1968; Hayashi, 1978a; Nonaka, 1991; Okubayashi, 1988). This section illustrates three qualitative studies, one involving the view of middle and junior Japanese managers and professionals regarding Japanese management, one about the critical analysis of Fukushima nuclear accident, and a case study exploring the Japanese video game industry and characters.

Managerial Insights from Middle and Junior Professionals

In order to gather insights from the younger generation of Japanese professionals, we conducted several interviews and dynamic group sessions in 2020, 2021, and 2022 with seventy-two professionals. They are mostly Japanese middle and junior managers and professionals from both small and large Japanese enterprises, as well some other Asian professionals who experienced Japanese management. Our main questions revolved around their understanding of Japanese management, to what extent its principles are still valid in their organizations, and whether there are any new elements in terms of organizational development.

The interviewees and dynamic group participants underlined the following elements as the most distinctive and continued practices in Japanese management: a seniority-based system for promotion and pay, a company-based union, job stability (security), and normative rules and standardization. While these traditional Japanese management practices persist even after decades of changes and organizational reforms, the participants also mentioned organizational trends in productivity improvements, like customer-oriented initiatives and proposals, intra-organizational structure and network for business operations, encouraging new ideas and initiatives, continuous training and learning, and transformation to an innovation-oriented organization. Some participants commented on the pressure put on large organizations to be role models in their respective industries for what concerns the employees' work–life balance, advocating not working during holidays or persuading staff to take paternity leave. A few of the participating individuals had worked in the same company since graduating, while others had had at least one job change. Some expressed interest in staying with the same company for the sake of job security, despite better positions in previous jobs, while others looked for challenges and higher pay.

In these large enterprises, we can generally observe continuity in long-term employment relationships with strong commitment, even though the professionals of the younger generation value learning-developmental opportunities along with job security. If only job security is guaranteed, without many opportunities for development, a young professional may prefer to look for positions in other sectors. The seniority-based system is still the prevalent mechanism in the enterprises as participants suggested. Yet, some organizations are moving from traditionally rigid personnel management toward more flexible human resources management, because they are under pressure to internationalize both for the purpose of market expansion – as the Japanese domestic market is shrinking due to the country's decreasing population – and owing to the need to attract international employees to fill the labor gap. Overall, the professionals who participated in our study believe that their organizations are still very traditional places, where incumbents follow rules and are risk-averse, but efforts in transformation are being stepped up, with annual innovation contests to encourage innovative behavior.

Contrasts and the coexistence of traditionalism and frontier transformation are evident. For instance, work–life balance (e.g., addressing the issue of traditionally long working hours), diversity (e.g., how to deal with international staff working in Japan), and gender equality (e.g., the role of women in the business sector) are some of the people-related issues that Japan's top-ranking enterprises need to deal with to meet society's current demands. Nonetheless, the embedded traditional values and culture are so strong that, as reported by one of the professionals interviewed, to ensure compliance with work–life balance regulations, a higher-level manager may have to call a subordinate on a holiday to ensure that the person is taking a rest instead of working. In another case, the human resources department may ask employees to take paternity leave to increase the company's indicators measuring work–life balance or gender equality. In spite of this, only two out of ten employees actually go on paternity leave, since rejecting such an offer is well perceived in general, easily justified by many pending tasks, and anyone seeking a promotion needs to take their image in the workplace into consideration and be in place when promotion opportunities arise. Another example given is that of compulsory two-year maternity leave regulations implemented by the organization, regardless of whether the female employees welcomed the decision. In certain cases, these employees even decided not to return to work out of shame because of the gossip about their long absence. Lastly, one of our female interviewees expressed concern about the possible restructuring of the company where she worked due to the economic downturn caused by COVID-19. As her spouse worked in the same organization, it seemed highly likely that she would be laid off instead of her husband.

The brainstorming activities during the dynamic group sessions revealed the deep-rooted beliefs of Japanese business professionals about the unique characteristics of Japanese management. The topics listed in what follows are not comprehensive but cover major Japanese management issues related to people, behavior, and human resources management: highly contextual culture, risk aversion, employment relations (e.g., labor union, long-term employment, group-based appraisal), group decision-making versus individual opinion, and other features, like seniority-based promotion, no (clear) job description, competitive but at the same time homogenous, collective, and silent culture.

Fukushima Nuclear Accident

As Gerdeman (2020) points out, citing the words of Takeuchi, Japanese people and firms are good at surviving crises, including natural and man-made disasters. Examples could be Naomi Hasegawa's family business selling toasted mochi in Kyoto, which has survived for more than one thousand years (Dooley and Ueno, 2020). As the country's population is strongly aware of and well prepared for disasters, it is no surprise that disaster management is widely studied by Japanese scholars. Regular training sessions are held nationwide, along with annual exhibitions and simulations in elementary schools to teach even the youngest children how to react in situations of flood, earthquake, tsunami, and so on. In a recent tsunami incident on January 15, 2022, the disaster/crisis-aware and prepared Japanese people in Iwate prefecture moved quickly to evacuate, when the tsunami caused by the Tonga volcano eruption hit the Pacific coast. Many said that they always keep in mind where to evacuate to in case of emergency, and a senior citizen commented that "it's a very good thing that young people were some of the first to evacuate" (Kyodo, 2022).

The nuclear accident that occurred at the Tokyo Electric Power Company's (TEPCO) Fukushima Daiichi Nuclear Power Plant, in the wake of the Great East Japan Earthquake on March 11, 2011, serves as a prime example for the analysis of crisis management in natural or man-made catastrophes. Kase, Nonaka, and Independent Panel (2012) describe in exhaustive detail the events that occurred at the Fukushima Daiichi Nuclear Power Station (NPS) between March 11, 2011 and March 24, 2011. First, the largest ever recorded earthquake (magnitude of 9.0) hit the Pacific coast area of northeastern Japan, followed by a tsunami in a series of seven waves engulfing 561 km². The Fukushima Daiichi NPS had six light boiling water reactors (BWR), which is the second most common type after the pressurized water reactor (PWR) type. A major difference between BWR and PWR is that BWR-type reactors have a simpler structure but the handling of radioactive materials is more difficult. Because the earthquake damaged the breakers and other circuitry, all the power supplied by the six lines connected to the Daiichi NPS stopped. Then, two tsunami waves, the first 4 m high and the second more than 7.5 m high,[2] flooded the Daiichi main buildings, which were licensed based on the assumption of a maximum 3.1 m high tsunami and the maximum design basis tsunami height was expected to be 3.1 to 3.7 m (Nuclear Emergency Response Headquarters, 2011). This rendered all six seawater pumps useless in releasing decay heat into the sea.

The subsequent occurrences caused different types of technical damage. Although the security system for processing the nuclear materials, the procedure to obtain energy, and other systems were still in place, a marginal problem in the construction design converted an unimaginably small percentage of probability into a disaster of reality with the tsunami. Gradual loss of control of the reactor stemmed from technical damage to the machinery, resulting in increased temperature. The construction design defects meant that the emergency plan could not work, as the tsunami destroyed the building's housing emergency materials. Robots and engineers worked at the Daiichi NPS fighting against the radioactivity to repair the reactor and make the systems work, while helicopters delivered water and other substances to keep the temperature stable. The construction, specifically designed to withstand earthquakes, also helped (Zarazúa, 2021).

The technical aspects of the event concerning nuclear energy have been widely discussed by specialists, but some scholars, like Kase, Canton and Zhang (2012), have focused on the managerial aspects: problem solving, the role of leadership, and learning and knowledge creation during the crisis.

---

[2] These heights refer to the initial major tsunamis arriving at Daiichi main buildings around 15:27, 41 minutes later than mainshock occurrence, according to the press conference of TEPCO on April 9, 2011 (Nuclear Emergency Response Headquarters, 2011: III-30).

Despite the unfortunate catastrophe created by the accident at the Fukushima Daiichi NPS, the intensive interactions, coordination, and interventions among people in the NPS and different stakeholders were able to reduce the extent of the disaster, though not without criticisms.

Most Japanese power structure studies have pointed out that Japanese people prefer consensus building in order to avoid unnecessary conflicts. Groupthink is adopted when a drive for consensus exists in such crisis situations, suppressing dissent and appraisal of alternatives in the decision-making process and excluding opposing ideas. Several situations that occurred in the case under discussion demonstrate this consensus approach in making hasty decisions, without sufficient information to perform a precise analysis, or in implementing actions without fluid communication with other parties involved. The presence of multiple leadership levels also complicated the decision-making process, from the Prime Minister Naoto Kan to the Ministry of Economy, Trade, and Industry (METI), the Nuclear and Industrial Safety Agency (NISA), the incumbent autonomous government in Fukushima, TEPCO top management, and the Director of Fukushima Daiichi, Masao Yoshida (see Figure 2).

The Fukushima Daiichi Nuclear Power Station accident shows the challenges of management in a critical disaster event, which is full of uncertainty, information ambiguity, complexity, and potential volatility. Questions have been raised concerning leadership, communication sufficiency, information flow and adequacy, knowledge integration, and crisis coping (Kase, Nonaka, and Independent Panel, 2012). According to the note of Kase, Canton and Zhang (2012), the Independent Investigation Commission on the Fukushima Daiichi Nuclear Accident (2012; 2014) states the importance of the advisory function by specialists in cases of large-scale technological failures: "The crisis management capability of the government was weak. The principal reason was that the

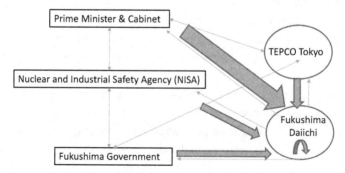

Figure 2 Multilevel leadership and decision-making in the Fukushima Daiichi event

secretariat at the Nuclear Emergency Headquarters did not function, namely, NISA did not live up to expectations." The analysis goes further and criticizes the fallacy of bureaucratic mechanisms in times of crisis when "decision-making depends on flexibility, adaptability, prioritization of issues, redundancy, top-down decision, etc."

Similarly, the assessment of Professor Nonaka from the Independent Independent Investigation Commission on the Fukushima Daiichi Nuclear Accident (2012; 2014) stresses the complexity of nuclear power generation as an advanced technology and continuous process, which requires analyses beyond the physical installations and machinery, also encompassing its under-lying cognition, values, behavior patterns, system, organizational culture, and so on (Kase, Canton, and Zhang, 2012). The fact that Fukushima Daiichi was part of a closed community precluded from exchanging knowledge with out-siders became the main cause of the crisis, resulting from a deterioration in knowledge and wisdom. While the multiple layers of communication channels and information filtering among different units caused delays in taking action, leadership also failed to assume responsibility. On the one hand, TEPCO's management and executives were too focused on complying with regulations, analyses, and planning, falling short of being truly well-rounded leaders. On the other hand, the Prime Minister's micromanagement of each individual phenom-enon hindered action. In an unprecedented crisis, or VUCA context, problems are often ill-defined and domain knowledge is scarce. Therefore, different levels of leadership may have to organize protocols, schemes, and communication channels on their own, coming up with many procedures from scratch (Kase, Nokana, and Independent Panel, 2012). Cognitive creativeness and open-mindedness are mandatory in this sense to integrate knowledge and wisdom.

The Fukushima Daiichi accident has prompted Japan and the world to funda-mentally review their entire energy and nuclear power policy. From the manager-ial perspective, it has provided a learning event to strengthen management and leadership for knowledge to flow in a flexible way, so as to achieve new knowledge creation. The rigidity of bureaucratic mechanisms within an organ-ization and beyond its boundaries, namely in the interorganization ecosystem, may be fatal in a critical event if domain knowledge is lacking. Interdisciplinary communication flows may enhance this knowledge and wisdom integration process to create new knowledge for solution providing in dynamic, uncertain, and ambiguous environments. A relatively effective management in the accident, albeit all the fallacies remain to be learned, has prevented the disaster from being worsened. The analysis pinpoints the key factors of leadership and learning along with the strong ethical and responsibility culture among all the stakeholders involved in the networked event to manage the knowledge flow.

Japanese Character-Based Video Game Industry

In this section we provide a case illustration concerning knowledge flow in the Japanese video game industry.[3] From tabletops to virtual reality, online gaming was estimated to reach 196 billion USD in revenue in 2022, as one of the fastest growing industries in the world (Jones, 2020). Internet gaming has skyrocketed in popularity in just a few decades thanks to the emergence and advancement of the online gaming industry, as well as the technical possibilities that will shape its future. The Japanese video game industry is definitely one of the most powerful sectors that have influenced the lives of many individuals around the world. Video gaming is also a major industry in Japan, featuring a number of key companies (e.g., Nintendo, Sega and Sony) and popular games and characters (e.g., *Super Mario Bros., Pac-Man, Donkey Kong, The Legend of Zelda,* and *Pokémon*; see a list of top Japanese video game companies in Table 3). The revenue of the online video game segment in Japan was projected to reach 18 billion USD in 2021, with annual growth of 7.13 percent and user penetration of 77.3 percent, to hit 85.8 percent by 2025, while the worldwide video game market was valued at 159 billion USD in 2020 and expected to reach 201 billion USD in 2023 (Statista, 2021a, b), not including physical video game sales and demo/trial versions.

Early Stages of the Global and Japanese Video Game Industry

The earliest precursor of a video game appeared with the patent for a "Cathode-Ray Tube Amusement Device" filed in 1947 and granted in 1948 in the United States, which described how players could use a controller to hit one or more targets. However, no evidence exists that any prototype was even built. Then came the 1950s' Nimrod and Higinbotham's *Tennis Game* and the 1960s' *Spacewar*, but these products did not have much commercial value (Herman, 2016). That is why Dabney (2016) claims that the video game industry was actually established with the creation of arcade video games by Syzygy/Atari in 1972.

The cofounder of Atari, Nolan Bushnell, started Atari Japan to import Atari's products, but the local market was reluctant to do business with his firm. Meanwhile, Japanese companies started to release their own video games to compete with Atari, exemplified by Sega and Taito in the early 1970s. Both were headquartered in Japan but founded for other business purposes by foreigners, American and Russian businessmen respectively. Sega made its

---

[3] This section is contributed by Zhang-Zhang, Y. and Morio, T., supported by Grant-in-Aid for Scientific Research (19K01926).

Table 3 Top Japanese video game companies

Name	Founding year	Year starting game business	Original business	Revenue (in bn ¥)
Sony	1946	1993 (Sony Interactive Entertainment, formerly SCE)	Electronics	8,999.4
Nintendo	1889	1977	Playing cards	1,758.9
Bandai Namco Entertainment	2006 (Bandai, 1950 and Namco, 1955)	1985 (Bandai) and 1960s (Namco)	Toys for Bandai and Amusement (for Namco)	740.9
Sega Sammy	2004 (Sega,1960 and Sammy, 1975)	1960 (Sega) and 1975 (Sammy)	Slot machines for Sega & Amusement Arcade Machines for Sammy	366.6
Square Enix	2003 (Enix, 1975 and Square, 1983)	1875	Publishing games (Enix), Computer game software (Square)	332.0
Konami	1969	1978	Jukebox rental and repair business	272.7
Koei Tecmo	2009 (Koei, 1978 and Tecmo, 1967)	1983 (Koei) and 1969 (Tecmo)	Personal computer sales (Koei), supplier of cleaning equipment (Tecmo)	42.6
Capcom	1983	1983	Digital content	0.8

Note: Revenue data is of fiscal year 2020, ending on March 31, 2021. 1JPY (¥) = 0.00906465 USD on March 31, 2021 as midmarket rates, according to www.xe.com.

first clone of Atari's *Pong*, called *Ping-Tron*, while Taito purchased Atari's used *Pong* machines, refurbished them, and distributed them as *Elepong*. Realizing that the importation process was costly, Taito started to produce its own *Pong* clones with additional features, for example *Soccer*, with an added twist, and *Davis Cup*, designed for up to four players (Herman, 2016).

The Japanese company Namco initially entered the video game industry to deal with the distribution of Atari games in Japan. As Atari's financial difficulties increased, Namco ended up acquiring Atari Japan, beating other competitors such as Sega and Taito. With the success of Atari's *Breakout*, Namco became one of Japan's leading video game companies (Kent, 2010). After the release of Taito's *Space Invaders*, the Japanese video game industry prospered in the 1970s and Namco turned its attention to developing proprietary video games. Having purchased NEC's old stock computers for employees to study, Namco released its first original game in 1978, *Gee Bee*. Despite not meeting expectations, this experience served to gain a space in the market and paved the way for Namco's next launches and hits, including *Galaxian* in 1979 and *Puck Man* (*Pac-Man* in North America) in 1980 (Koyama, 2005). To celebrate *Pac-Man*'s thirtieth Anniversary, Namco Networks (2010) announced that the franchise had surpassed 30 million paid transactions in the United States on Brew ® apps.

Home video game consoles were first marketed in Japan roughly two years after they appeared in the United States. In 1977 Japanese companies (e.g., Bandai) released their own consoles, which were similar to the American Odyssey console by Magnavox, launched in 1975. Also in 1977, Nintendo released its own home console with the help of Mitsubishi Electric, due to its lack of skilful engineers in home game designing. Soon the inexpensive model of Nintendo's Color TV-Game 6 achieved large success and the company controlled 70 percent of the home console business (Herman, 2016; Sheff, 1993).

The early 1980s saw the peak of the golden age of arcade video games, although many video game publishers had gone bankrupt by 1984 (Kohler, 2016). Yet, the US video game market crashed, since American enterprises like Atari, Coleco, and Mattel were not able to keep up with industry developments. Nintendo's NAVS Famicom video game system, with Japanese video games translated into English, revived the US market in 1985/1986. Indeed, the unit that Nintendo America marketed was called Nintendo Advanced Video System (NAVS), not Famicom. It was completely wireless and had an advanced system that American firms could not compete with. It was also impossible for American video games to compete with Japanese games like Nintendo's *Super Mario Bros.* (Herman, 2016; Kohler, 2016).

Japanese Characters in the Video Game Industry

Though video games were initially introduced into the Japanese market by Americans, Japanese firms soon saw the potential of this business and started their own game designing. In spite of a slight time gap, Japanese enterprises were able to catch up fast and even developed titles with better features to compete first in the Japanese market and then in that of the United States. Their later success in the United States was also achieved thanks to better innovation in hardware and video game design and programming. The video game industry prospered in Japan, with the popularization of Taito's *Space Invaders* in 1978, and the subsequent success of Japanese enterprises made some games so widely known that they entered popular culture (Kohler, 2016). The Japanese video game sector is the exception to what Kerr (2001) calls the fall of modern Japan, stating that Japan does not lead in any single field despite maintaining competent standards in many industries.

Kohler (2016) partly attributes the success of video games to the unique culture of Japan and its love for cartoons and comics. Schodt (1983) refers to young Japanese (today's middle-aged Japanese) as *shikaku sedai* (visual generation), who consider comics a common language, emphasize images, and have no bias against this medium. Indeed, in the 1980s, many talented young people actually became video game designers. This feature is also reflected in the medium of the video game, which Herz (1997) describes as an easy translation of the Japanese way of drawing characters in *manga* (comics), when their graphic resolution did not yet allow representing characters with adult proportions. Kohler argues that the pictographic language of written Japanese is the source of Japan's prevalent image culture, whereas in the Western world picture books and comic books are seen as entertainment for children. While some American game designers criticized Japanese video games and predicted their failure in the United States (Bloom, 1982), reality turned out to be quite different. With the release of Taito's *Space Invaders* in 1978, Japanese video game producers quickly took over the industry (Herman, 2016). The later success of Nintendo in both hardware (consoles) and software (games) led the Japanese video game industry to prosper further and, by 1990, Nintendo had replaced Atari in the position of market leader both in the United States and globally (Kohler, 2016).

The success of Nintendo in the video game industry is probably related to its original business of making playing cards and the creative potential released in the process of refining home console products, video game design, and character creation. Shigeru Miyamoto, the creator of *Donkey Kong, Super Mario Bros.*, and *The Legend of Zelda*, described Nintendo as an interesting company when he first joined. Initially seeking a career as a *manga* artist, he took interest in video games later (Paumgarten, 2010). Before he directed the *Donkey Kong* project for its release in 1981, it was programmers and engineers who were responsible for game design. In many cases, the Nintendo engineers even drew the pictures and composed the music, with no artist involved in the process (Kohler, 2016). The design of *Donkey Kong* led by Miyamoto created the first real video game storyline, different from the earlier maze and shooter games common at the time (Sheff, 1999). Retrospectively, Miyamoto reflected that he had unconsciously created *Donkey Kong* based on his love for Japanese manga (Kohler, 2016).

The next title, *Super Mario Bros.*, was also about game play, with running/jumping/climbing actions like *Donkey Kong* but, rather than merely achieving a high score, for the first time players were tasked with completing the story as the goal of the game, in order to discover what happened when you saved the princess. The stories and characters of *Mario Bros* and its sequels have been turned into comic books, movies, TV shows, and novels that have enjoyed wide popularity and success. Miyamoto's creation of *The Legend of Zelda* in 1986 followed the same game design pattern of a storyline but its scenarios were much richer. It was so complex and expansive, in comparison with earlier games, that it was the first time the player could, and needed to save the game and start again from where he/she had left off because the adventure could not be finished in one sitting (Kohler, 2016).

As it became customary for the story mode to accompany game play, game designers worked harder on story writing, and this trend lasted for about ten years. Then, the new trend of role-playing games (RPGs) emerged with the launch of the *Dragon Quest* series for Nintendo's Famicom in 1990 by Enix (later Square Enix), a Japanese software publisher and video game holding company (Herman, 2016; Kohler, 2016). The software coevolved with the hardware in the video game industry, bringing about innovative features and technology incorporation each time. In spite of the initial success of the Atari Video Computer System (later renamed 2600), the poor sales performance of 1993's Jaguar, the only available 64-bit interactive media entertainment system, made it the last home console that Atari produced and the last by an American manufacturer until Microsoft launched its Xbox in 2001 (Herman, 2016; Kohler, 2016). Today, Nintendo's Switch and Sony's PlayStation are two of the three major competitors in the home console business around the world, along with Microsoft's Xbox. Computer gaming and mobile gaming have also increased their share in the internationalized digital society, and online multiple-player games are another characteristic feature. Mobile games popularized in the last decade have enjoyed remarkable growth given the technological improvements in smartphone technology. For example, the mobile game *Pokémon Go*, a recent global success launched in 2016, has classic Japanese characters (the first Pokémon game was released as early as 1996) and employs augmented reality (AR). Given the love of Japanese people for *manga*, anime, and video games, the cross-media merger of the content business seems a natural evolution.

Licensing of Characters: Innovation Ecosystem

Japanese pop culture content, such as *manga*, animation films (anime), and video games, is nowadays widely recognized and appreciated all over the world. In particular, the unique appearance of Japanese characters has attracted fans from across the globe. One of the remarkable features of the Japanese content business is its wide cross-media extension, especially for what concerns character-related intellectual property (IP). The expansion of the character business has been driven by cross-media development across television, films, and books, as well as by the development of products such as toys, stationery, and other items.

The management and operation of copyright and licensing are crucial to the expansion of these segments. The first full-scale cross-media development of a character in Japan after World War II is said to have been Astro Boy (Tetsuwan Atom), an animated television series that began airing in 1963. The copyright holders of Astro Boy began to control the quality of the character's products by marking those that they approved as authentic and withholding any other.

Since the 1990s, companies that own the copyright on specific works or characters have taken a strategic lead in developing the business rather than leaving it entirely to the companies that make the products, as cross-media, product, and service development is all part of the character's worldview.

Pokémon is one of the most successful examples of a business that has expanded not only in Japan but also internationally, thanks to a range of mobile games, manga and anime, related goods, card games, events, smartphone applications, official stores and cafes, and social contribution activities. This business development is guided by a consortium of companies, led by the *Pokémon* copyright management company, Pokémon Co (Hatayama and Kubo, 2000).

Another example of a successful product enjoying worldwide popularity is Hello Kitty, a *kawaii* (cute) idol created by Sanrio's illustrator Yuko Shimizu in 1974. The turning point was in 2008 when, after joining Sanrio, Rehito Hatoyama benchmarked Disney and Sesame Street characters and determined that Hello Kitty could achieve similar levels of success. He convinced the Sanrio management to adopt a licensing model instead of the traditional design, make, and sell approach. In this licensing model, other companies can obtain the rights to create and sell Hello Kitty-themed products in exchange for a percentage of product sales as royalties. By focusing on IP management, not only did Sanrio improve its efficiency by reducing production, inventory, and retail costs through the outsourcing of manufacturing and distribution, but it also leveraged the creative capabilities of other external stakeholders around the world in designing and developing Hello Kitty products. This open innovation licensing strategy brought significant changes to Sanrio, including an increase in Hello Kitty licensees from 760 in 2007 to 1,800 in 2011 and in operating profit from 53 million USD in 2007 to 237 million USD in 2011. In 2014, Sanrio became the sixth biggest licensor in the world, with 50,000 products and 6.5 billion USD of licensing retail sales. Among these, Hello Kitty accounted for 75 percent of its annual operating profit. Aware of the threat posed by e-commerce, in the second half of the 2010s Sanrio introduced new ways to engage with consumers and new kinds of characters, for example cross-sector ventures in the restaurant business (e.g., Hello Kitty Smile restaurant, Hello Kitty Cafe), "experiential" ventures like educational programs about healthy eating and sustainability, Hello Kitty theme parks, and a joint licensing agreement with Mattel (IP owner of Barbie, Fisher-Price, and Thomas & Friends) to design and market characters of both companies (Craig, 2020).

Recently, a new approach has emerged that is different from the strategic cross-media development by the copyright holders seen for Pokémon and Hello Kitty. In this approach, the derivative works of the fans are the driving force behind cross-media development, as shown in the following two examples. The first is Hatsune Miku, a virtual singer software that was released by Crypton Future Media in 2007 and continues to evolve. Before Hatsune Miku, there had been several virtual singer software releases, but its main distinguishing feature is that, in addition to being a music creation tool, it is personified by an idol-like character.

One of the interesting aspects of Hatsune Miku is that her songs are often used as a basis for cross-media development. For example, the song "Senbonzakura" was contributed by a vocaloid creator, Kurousa P. (Avex Marketing Inc., 2013). The song became popular on the internet, and novels and manga inspired by it were published. The world of Senbonzakura gradually took shape, became more and more concrete, and was eventually developed into musicals and kabuki plays.

Although the copyright holder, Crypton Future Media, has licensed the characters for this development, the media development was not planned strategically, but rather happened spontaneously among the fans. The authors of both the original compositions and derivative works, such as novels and comics, have contributed to the creation of this universe, which is characterized by a sort of open innovation, with different stakeholders voluntarily participating in the ecosystem (Koyama, 2013).

In the case of Hatsune Miku, a different licensing strategy has been adopted than with Pokémon. Crypton Future Media, the copyright holder, has created the Piapro Character License, flexible licensing guidelines that make it easier for fans to create derivative works using Hatsune Miku, including not only music but also character art and manga. It is a simplified process that merely involves an online license application (Crypton Future Media, 2020).

Another example is Touhou Project, a collection of video games and music by the amateur game creator group Shanghai Alice Gengaku-dan (2015) (also called Team Shanghai Alice), led by Ota Junya (aka ZUN). The main characters of this series of shooting games are two girls, the shrine maiden Reimu Hakurei and the witch Marisa Kirisame. Like Hatsune Miku, Touhou Project encompasses a wide range of business activities: video games by third parties or coterie circles, publications such as manga, illustrations, and novels, fan events, figurines, collaborations with department stores, and even a fan-run hotel. The group behind Touhou Project has also established guidelines that allow free creation by fans.

The common trait of Hatsune Miku and Touhou Project is that cross-media development has been driven by the secondary creations of fans. In other words, the secondary creative activities of fans have expanded these universes into many different genres, which has led to business growth. The fans are also consumers of content, so they create what they want, which contributes to the expansion of a business that is less prone to failure, that is, it is designed to be "sellable."

From Astro Boy to Pokémon, Japanese writers and creators provided their works to readers and fans in a one-way fashion. In cross-media development, the authors and the copyright managers still provide content unilaterally. However, fans have begun to participate in the cross-media development of works through secondary creation, contributing to the business expansion of the world of their favorite characters. Examples such as Hatsune Miku and the Touhou Project are truly a testament to the development of digital technology and the internet. The widespread use of digital creation tools and the sharing of assets has dramatically lowered the bar for creation, allowing more and more fans to join in the creative process.

Character copyright holders will play a role not only in offering their characters to fans but also in providing an open platform for fans to create and enjoy the world of their characters together, including through derivative works. Until now, the character business has been about unifying and fixing the image of characters through licensing. An open platform, on the contrary, gives diversity to the interpretation and representation of characters, expanding both their universe and market.

5 People Centric Innovation Ecosystem

Section 4 discussed the coexistence of traditional Japanese management and modernization in contemporary Japanese enterprises, the need for knowledge and wisdom for new knowledge creation in an uncertain and ambiguous scenario such as a crisis like the Fukushima nuclear accident, as well as the constant innovation occurring in a cross-sector context like Japan's character-based video game industry. Continuous adaptation to the external environment or even taking the lead in changing their industries through innovation is necessary for firms to survive and prosper. The video game industry saw the fall of Atari, once itself synonymous with video games, because it could not compete innovatively and keep up with the shift from arcade video games to home consoles, led by Japanese firms. Atari's last home console product, Jaguar, manufactured in partnership with IBM, had such an advanced hardware system that there was a lack of compatible software when it was released in 1993, turning it into little more than memory rather than a game console (Kohler, 2016). The game console industry is closely intertwined with the development of game software, the computer industry, and market adoption. Moreover, in today's reality we can observe broader fuzziness and intersections among the sectors of video games, home consoles, personal computers (PCs), and other entertainment and technology businesses. The video game industry, as a creative industry, has innovation at its core but it is also an ecosystem strongly tied to different interactive stakeholders, intermingling with components of other business ecosystems. The creativity embedded in people, as knowledge workers, is at the centre of this ecosystem's functionality. In this section, we argue for a people centric innovation ecosystem, continuing with our illustration of Japanese enterprises.

Business Ecosystem and Innovation Ecosystem

An ecosystem is a community of living organisms and nonliving components interacting over time and space as a system, along with other organisms and adopting by themselves, from an ecological approach (Smith and Smith, 2012). The ecosystem construct has gained prominence in the work of academics and practitioners (Adner and Kapoor, 2010). The review by Bassis and Amellini (2018) identifies Rothschild (1990) as the earliest scholar to use an analogy between business and ecosystem; whereas Pilinkienė and Mačiulis (2014) for the three analogies – industrial ecosystem, digital business ecosystem, and entrepreneurship ecosystem – are the best known. Borrowing this ecological conceptualization and bringing it into the field of business and management, different dimensions have been explored. For instance, some scholars demonstrate the fierce competition existing in business environments (Moore, 1993, 1996), others specify the transdisciplinary perspective in services (Lusch, Vargo, and Gustafsson, 2016) or identify institutional complexity as a driver for innovation in services (Siltaloppi, Koskela-Huotari, and Vargo, 2016). Other academics refer to competition in terms of technological standards in Industry 4.0 (Jiang et al., 2020) or to coopetition in an innovation ecosystem with knowledge transfer (Bacon, Williams, and Davies, 2020).

Owing to globalization and technological development and progress, SMEs have greater chances to survive, be successful, and compete with large multinationals. This may arise from competitive advantages in a specific niche segment, as SMEs are often more flexible in organization and management or use digital platforms providing alternative advantages. Undoubtedly, globalization and digitization offer more room for entrepreneurship and creativity for SMEs to compete with traditional large corporations, burdened by heavier bureaucratic structures and formalized processes. In turn, this requires traditional large multinationals to create corporate entrepreneurship to renew and reinnovate themselves. In today's open and free market, businesses and industries are often divided into a large number of segments specialized in different products, services, and technologies (Bassis and Amellini, 2018). Such a multitude of actors in the system creates a high degree of interactions among firms involved in the design, research, development, manufacturing, marketing, distribution, and post-sales services of a single product (e.g., Iansiti and Levien, 2004). Focusing on the Japanese context, Startups (2020) states that, to overcome these new challenges stemming from industrial and social structural changes, Japanese companies need to reform their business model from the principle of self-sufficiency to greater openness and collaboration, in order to create innovation and address social issues such as depopulation and aging population.

Citing the words of Victor Hwang (2014), Gobble (2014) declares "It is not a fad" when talking about the phenomenon of business ecosystems. Indeed, the term ecosystem has become "the next big business buzzword" based on how much its usage has increased in the last ten years. On February 5, 2022, a general Google search returned 2,390,000 results for "business ecosystem" and 3,630,000 results for "innovation system." A specific Google Scholar search yielded 21,900 results for "business ecosystem" and 24,900 results for "innovation ecosystem." A more professional academic database like the Web of Science (WoS) featured in its Core Collection 873 articles on "business ecosystem" starting from 1993 and 912 articles on "innovation ecosystem" starting from 2003. Both terms display an increasing trend in terms of quality research publications (see Figure 3).

The WoS search results refer to Moore (1993) as the earliest journal article on business ecosystems, while the first publications on innovation ecosystems are two conference papers published in 2003, both about regional (technological) innovation ecosystems. So, the first truly impactful journal publication on

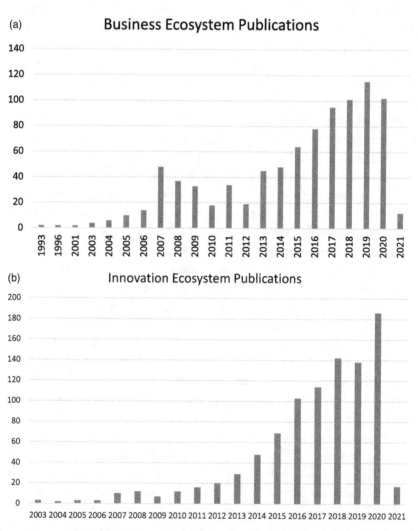

Figure 3 Publication trends of "business ecosystem" and "innovation ecosystem" per year

innovation ecosystems is by Adner (2006) and has the merit of combining the concepts of innovation strategy and innovation ecosystem. Nonetheless, Bassis and Amellini (2018) conclude that the concept of innovation ecosystem was first proposed by Moore (1993), given its emphasis on innovation in the business ecosystem conceptualization. Although the term "innovation ecosystem" itself does not appear in the text by Moore (1993), the term "innovation" is mentioned twenty-three times in the paper.

According to Moore (1993: 76), a business ecosystem is an economic community, and he regards a company "not as a member of a single industry but as part of a business ecosystem that crosses a variety of industries." Moreover, "companies co-evolve capabilities around a 'new' innovation: they work cooperatively and competitively to support new products, satisfy customer needs, and eventually incorporate the next round of innovations." Even though the definitions of business ecosystem and innovation ecosystem differ, a clear and strong tie between the two can be observed, showing that innovation is an inherent feature of business ecosystems. Conversely, the notion of innovation ecosystem by definition places more emphasis on innovative aspects, which Adner (2006: 99) refers to as "the collaborative arrangements through which firms combine their individual offerings into a coherent, customer-facing solution."

The Evolution of Innovation Ecosystems

Emerging as a promising approach in the literature on strategy, innovation, and entrepreneurship (de Vasconcelos Gomes, Figueiredo Facin, Salerno, and Ikenami, 2018), the concept of innovation ecosystem was reviewed by Arora, Belenzon, and Patacconi (2019) in the US context. Its first usage is traced back to as early as 1870, with three stages of evolution: early development of the US scientific–innovation complex (1870–1940), the age of big science (1940–1980) and open innovation, and the demise of the large corporate lab (1980 to date). What we mean by innovation ecosystem in the current state mostly coincides with this third stage as an open mode, in which the contribution of large firms to R&D has declined and the proportion of SMEs has grown. Venture-backed, small-sized start-ups have played a disproportionately large role in this innovation process as distinctive innovators (Kaplan and Lerner, 2010). In this sense, Japan's history in open innovation is not as long as that of the United States. During the 2000s, Japan had very little venture capital and limited investments in start-ups, whereas more partnerships between large companies with real assets and start-ups with capabilities to generate new business models are currently expected (Startups, 2020).

However, considering the intertwined view of the innovation ecosystem and the system of innovation (SI) found in another review work by Bassis and Amellini (2018), we can observe that the SI concept is believed to have emerged in the late 1980s to describe the congruence in Japanese society, in which the private and public sectors interact and initiate activities related to new technologies through import, modification, and diffusion (Freeman, 1987; Soete, Verspagen, and Weel, 2009). In any case, from an academic point of view, the evolutionary path of an innovation ecosystem very much depends on its definition; otherwise, it would be a never-ending meaningless debate. Indeed, at present there is no commonly agreed framework or definition for it. De Vasconcelos Gomes et al. (2018) list some scholarly definitions in various contexts, at different levels, using different labels, focuses, meanings, and purposes. Some examples to illustrate this complex scenario are digital innovation ecosystem (e.g., Rao and Jimenez, 2011; Chae, 2019), national or regional innovation ecosystem (e.g., Fukuda and Watanabe, 2008; Suseno and Standing, 2018), enterprises' innovation ecosystem (Huang et al., 2019), entrepreneurial innovation ecosystem (Guerrero and Martínez-Chávez, 2020), open innovation ecosystem (e.g., Chesbrough et al., 2014; Kvedaravičienė, 2019; Randhawa et al., 2021; Xie and Wang, 2021), hub ecosystem (Nambisan and Baron, 2013), and platform-based ecosystem (e.g., Gawer, 2014).

The exhaustive studies by both Bassis and Armellini (2018) and de Vasconcelos Gomes et al. (2018) include the concept of business ecosystem within an innovation ecosystem literature review. For instance, de Vasconcelos Gomes et al. (2018) employ both terms as keywords for topic searches in the WoS database, proposing the following reasons: (1) the notion of innovation ecosystem is defined based on the notion of business ecosystem in the management field; (2) some scholars regard business ecosystem as synonymous with innovation ecosystem, though some others do not; (3) there is no clear distinction between the conceptual evolution of the two ideas in the literature. In this inclusive interpretation, the study of innovation ecosystems can be traced back to an earlier time when the term business ecosystem came into use, or even further. Moore (1993) again becomes the pioneer in proposing a business ecosystem for innovation in the field of management, arguing for the frameworks related to networks, like strategic alliances and virtual organizations, and the need for managers to understand the relations between organizations and changes. This network view of the innovation ecosystem is followed by Iansiti and Levien (2004), who emphasize loosely connected networks of entities, and by Basole and Karla (2011), who define an ecosystem as a networked system containing a set of objects like actors, namely nodes tied to one another. In this sense, Japanese corporate network systems have been widely studied in the management field, looking at the distinctive network patterns of Japanese industrial organizations, including *keiretsu*, like Dai-Ichi Kangyo Bank (DKB, now Mizuho), Mitsubishi, Mitsu, Fuji, and Sumitomo (e.g., Bhappu, 2000; Gerlach, 1992). Besides regarding the network as a central feature, de Vasconcelos Gomes et al. (2018) also identify the following themes in the analysis: open innovation and product platform, strategic management, evolutionary economics, organization studies, as well as the ecosystem, business ecosystem, and innovation constructs.

Innovation Ecosystem Features

Merging the commonalities of innovation ecosystem and business ecosystem, de Vasconcelos Gomes et al. (2018) note five ecosystem features: (1) it is composed of interconnected and interdependent network actors; (2) it may be led by a keystone actor or a platform leader; (3) it is built on a platform; (4) ecosystem members encounter both cooperation and competition in the system; (5) it has a life cycle after the coevolution process.

To analyze an innovation ecosystem, characterized by more explicit interdependencies (Adner and Kapoor, 2010), it is necessary to identify firstly who the actors in its network are and then their roles. According to Iansiti and Levien (2004), Lee and Shin (2018), and Moore (1993), a typical business ecosystem comprises a few prominent actors as keystones and dominators and many smaller ones as complementary and niche players, as exemplified in the innovative fintech ecosystem (Zhang-Zhang, Rohlfer, and Rajasekera, 2020). Different stakeholders or network actors make up the ecosystem, including a focal firm, customers, suppliers, distributors, outsourcing firms, makers of related products or services, technology providers, a host of other organizations, and complementary innovators (de Vasconcelos Gomes et al., 2018; Iansiti and Levien, 2004). Other complementors may be regulatory agencies and media outlets, with less immediate effect but prevailing long-term influence on the business and innovation ecosystem (Iansiti and Levien, 2004), or corporate-sponsored ventures and independent entrepreneurs (Zahra and Nambisan, 2012). Zahra and Nambisan (2012) observe that these actors can be a group of companies or entities but also individuals.

The keystone actor (Iansiti and Levien, 2004) or platform leader (Gawer and Cusumano, 2008) assumes a leadership role in the innovation ecosystem, setting the goals, outlining the innovation platform, and exerting influence over other members of the community (Nambisan and Baron, 2013). The ecosystem leader is often a well-established large firm (Iansiti and Levien, 2004), though this is not necessarily always true given the dynamics of digital society and internet empowerment, which may drive the rapid growth of a relatively small firm and turn it into a giant over a short period of time. Rong (2011) classifies the actors and roles in terms of ecosystem life cycle: initiator (building the community through a platform), specialist (adding value to the core community), and adopter (developing products following the initiator and codesigning the platform with the specialist). Zhang-Zhang, Rohlfer, and Rajasekera (2020) also underline the evolution of the fintech ecosystem and business model innovations, the fuzzy boundaries of industries, with cross-sector players, and the ambiguity of the stakeholders' roles.

An innovation ecosystem is built on a common platform, shared among the community members via a set of tools, services, and technologies. All the members also share the destiny of the platform, regardless of their weight (Iansiti and Levien, 2004). The case of arcade video games, whose decline affected all ecosystem members without exceptions, shows that an ecosystem has a lifecycle of birth, emerging, expanding/diversifying, converging, consolidating/leadership, and renewing, or self-renewal (Moore, 1993; Rong, 2011). As illustrated in Section 4, Atari was the dominant player in the arcade ecosystem community, while most Japanese enterprises operated around it as distributors or imitators. During the life of an innovation ecosystem, community members may compete for survival, collaborate to develop the common objective of the network, or even pursue coopetition for critical knowledge transfer (Bacon, Williams, and Davies, 2020). The innovativeness of Japanese enterprises, in the creation of both hardware (home consoles) and software (story-based video games with characters), has revolutionized the video game ecosystem, renewing and expanding its community to include sophisticated software developers, content publishers, and high-tech companies involved in the metaverse business.

In a heterogeneous market, an interconnected and continuously evolving community and its actors may take on specific roles, cocreate value (Lusch, Vargo, and Gustafsson, 2016; Siltaloppi, Koskela-Huotari, and Vargo, 2016), and evolve depending on their development and innovative capabilities for existential survival, renewing the ecosystem or initiating a new one. Nintendo did so with the video game ecosystem and the same is true for Sony, which strategically mobilized ecosystem effects in entertainment content in the late 1980s. Sony's acquisition of CBS Records and Columbia Pictures reinforced sales of hardware devices, like Betamax VCRs and Walkman cassette players. However, Sony kept this ecosystem largely closed, refusing, for instance, to license Michael Jackson's music to non-Sony devices to generate royalty revenues. Most of all, the paradigmatic shift brought about by the introduction of the iPod in 2001 and of the iPhone in 2007 greatly diminished Sony's value.

With PC and online games evolving fast, the lack of a platform or cloud service exposed Sony's vulnerability, vis-à-vis Microsoft's Xbox (Givens, 2022). Alternatively, the intentional actions and coordination efforts of managers and entrepreneurs may modify the construct and composition of the ecosystem, leading or adapting to changes in the business environment (Teece, 2016). Probably, the latter may be less discussed in the innovation ecosystem literature regarding this strategic intent and people management for the adaption or modification of an innovation ecosystem, as the essential functionality and activities of an ecosystem consist in the flow of technology, information, and knowledge among people, enterprises, and institutions to nurture and enhance the innovation processes.

People as Knowledge Workers and Innovation

Strategic thinking and entrepreneurship influence each other in an ecosystem cycle to sustain and even create innovation (Zahra and Nambisan, 2012). As knowledge and innovation come to be the center of the strategic issue of the firm as the fundamental for the firm's competitive advantages, innovation or knowledge creation is a strategic resource for firm prosperity (Drucker, 1993). People, or knowledge workers (Zhang-Zhang et al., 2022), including managers, IT staff, or any employee, are the embedded subjects to carry out strategic thinking and entrepreneurial activities to foster the occurrence of innovation in a business ecosystem, which is especially relevant in a VUCA context where dynamism is high.

Innovation refers not only to technological innovation but also to organizational innovation or administrative innovation (Kimberly and Evanisko, 1981; Martin, 2012), strategic innovation (Grant, 2016; Markides, 1997), and business mode innovation (Girotra and Netessine, 2014). All these different dimensions of innovation could be critical for the survival of a community and the competitiveness of a business ecosystem. A humanistic approach to knowledge management and innovation is a central strategic issue (Nonaka and Takeuchi, 2021; Zhang, Zhou, and McKenzie, 2013), since an organization can be viewed as a platform and context for individuals to innovate and diffuse knowledge via socialization at multiple levels (Nonaka, 1994). The innovative capabilities of an organization are based on the individuals' creativity across different levels, depending on processes, structure, motivation, and strategic alignment. In an open environment, both intra-organizational and interorganizational knowledge transfer and innovation processes are critical to attain strong performance (Liu and Zhang, 2014).

In the dynamic theories of knowledge management, individuals are regarded as leading actors and environmental change agents (Nonaka, 2011) that play a critical role in the nexus of an ecosystem's community development. From a knowledge worker's perspective, a people centric view is especially commended, since it stimulates dynamic capability formation in highly dynamic environments, induced not only by disruptive technologies (e.g., digitization), unpredictable crises (e.g., Fukushima Nuclear Accident), and high-velocity emerging markets (e.g., postwar Japan), but also by simultaneous effects triggered by multiple inducers. Four strategic dynamic constituents – leadership, culture, learning, and networking – are holistically integrated to help acquire, transfer, and create knowledge relevant for the sustainable development of the firm (Zhang-Zhang et al., 2022). The review of human resources mechanisms in relation to innovation consists of nine items: (1) innovation-oriented vision and culture as corporate strategic orientation, (2) recruitment with diversified competencies, (3) empowerment-focused job design, (4) cross-functional and employee suggestion-based communication system, (5) holistic training development, (6) formative performance-enhanced appraisal, (7) mixed (intrinsic and extrinsic) reward system, (8) long-term commitment with diverse opportunities in career development and job stability, and (9) collaboration with intelligent external resources (Zhang et al., 2013).

People Centric Japanese Management

In relation to what was argued in Sections 2 and 3, we can observe that, despite its evolutions and adaptations, the essence of Japanese management is people centric. The popular work by Johnson/Pascale and Ouchi (1974: 61) features an interview with an American manager in a Sony Corporation plant in the United States, who says: "You get a feeling around here that they care about people, whereas in my previous work experience with US companies they cared only about output and meeting the profit projection." This leads Johnson/Pascale and Ouchi to state that Japanese-style management contains elements of caring about people and other intrinsic characteristics that result in its high and healthy performance. This people centricity supports the business and, indeed, Sony's purpose is to "fill the world with emotion, through the power of creativity and technology." Takeda (2022) describes Sony's open culture, along with digitization, using the words of Akio Morita: "We encourage that every participant in a meeting to talk freely, just like a top management in our company."

The bottom-up or middle-up-down decision-making process of Japanese management with both vertical and horizontal diffusion and communication, via either digitized or traditional channels (Takeda, 2022), facilitates strategic people management by means of transformative leadership, entrepreneurial networking, innovative culture, and strategic learning (Zhang-Zhang et al., 2022). In a supposed way to make to function, Japanese senior managers play the role of facilitators, not commanders, dialectically challenging the initiatives proposed by subordinates until merit is perceived (Johnson/Pascale and Ouchi, 1974). The controversial aspect is that this may turn into *tatemae*, as pointed out by Yang (1984). While innovative ideas and initiatives can be proposed and rigorously debated in pursuit of improved solutions, the risk is that overhomogenous employee profiles with little diversity may limit the sources of creativity to spark innovation. The traditional common practice of recruiting recent graduates from universities and training them on the job continues today. In addition, limited external hiring of middle managers restricts the employees' diversity portfolio, which may be against item (2) earlier, namely recruitment with diversified competencies. While this contributes to a united force working toward the same strategic goals, it may eventually have some negative consequences, due to the lack of diversified competencies. Diversity needs to be part of organizational culture; otherwise, hard policies may not function without the existence of soft cement. Lastly, diversity may not necessarily refer to gender diversity, but also to international diversity, background diversity, and diversity of any other kind.

Another contributor to the dysfunction of bottom-up initiatives could be Japan's highly contextual culture, in which employees are expected to know their company well and thus "understand what the company wants you to do even if they don't tell you what to do" (Johnson and Ouchi, 1974, p. 63). In the past, this common background had its advantages in effective low-cost communication; however, its double-edged effects have also turned it against itself. One example is that, in order to have a harmonious relationship, subordinates may guess what their bosses expect and put forward proposals that are in line with the higher executives' thoughts; yet, this may not necessarily release the authentic creativity of the employees, thereby failing to lead to improved solutions. In such a case, any bottom-up decision becomes a mere bureaucratic process, wasting a large amount of time and resources, and, worst of all, it delays actual decision-making to respond to the market and meet customer demands. Unfortunately, in today's accelerated globalization and digitalization, the latter is of paramount importance. On the other hand, in a diverse environment, for example referring to international diversity, managers from cultural contexts other than that of Japan may not necessarily understand the subtleties of this harmonious, highly contextual culture or, despite comprehending the cultural context in general, they may not be able to capture every single detail and interpret it in an appropriate manner. All of this may ultimately lead to a dysfunctional managerial process.

The traditional recruitment method of focusing on homogenous graduates provides continuity in on-the-job training practices as a necessary part of the overall Japanese people management chain. In addition to other training opportunities and job rotation practises to develop generalist profiles, this appears to have a positive link to item (5) presented earlier, namely holistic training development, which positively influences innovative people management. Nevertheless, some dynamic groups outcomes (as introduced in Section 4) also comment on the ambiguous or entirely absent job descriptions in many Japanese organizations, which may be a drawback, negatively influencing item (3) of innovative people management, namely empowerment-focused job design.

The traditional lifetime employment system brought about a glorious innovation period for Japanese enterprises, given the mutual long-term commitment between the individual and the firm, which allowed risk-taking in the innovative process. While this corresponds to item (8) of innovative people management, namely long-term commitment with diverse opportunities in career development and job stability, lifetime employment became a heavy burden for companies during periods of downturn, even though numerous mechanisms were deployed to release this tension. A secondary effect is that some large enterprises currently have a batch of aging employees that were recruited in the 1980s and have been staying with them ever since in secure jobs. This is a double-edged sword: while these permanent employees have contributed to firm growth and knowledge accumulation over time, they are also poorly adapted to the digitalized systems of Industry 4.0. Instead of the initial purpose of encouraging knowledge workers to innovate without risking their job security, lifetime employment is currently compromising and seeking for consensus. Some interviewees remark that the aging employees in their companies have difficulty utilizing digital tools and there is strong resistance to digital transformation. Partly thanks to COVID-19, this phenomenon has decreased since COVID-19 lockdowns provided no alternatives to working with digital instruments.

The double-edged effects of lifetime employment and the seniority-based system cause many Japanese organizations to have a large number of older employees that occupy relevant managerial or middle-level positions. This situation hinders reforms aimed at more flexible human resources management policies, given the bottom-up or middle-up-down decision-making traditions, and makes it difficult to attract young, talented employees due to limited career development opportunities. A few of our interviewees state that some colleagues decided to move to another company because they did not see any promotion opportunity in the short and medium term, while others have chosen to wait a little longer and see how things develop. Despite calls for flexible human resources management practices since the 1990s, the pace of change is still rather slow. In this regard, the younger generations of employees underline the challenges of item (7), namely mixed (intrinsic and extrinsic) reward system.

Although the bottom-up decision-making process and participative management set the environment for employees to perceive self-realization through tasks and initiatives – and, indeed, most of the interviewees demonstrate their commitment to their organizations – some comments during the brainstorming session raised the concern that promotion appears to be the only means to increase salary. Due to the presence of many aging workers, the recruitment of mid-career employees also occurs to strengthen the age profile of businesses. However, in traditional Japanese enterprises, these mid-career new recruits may need to start from scratch, as if they were fresh graduates, since they may not know the company well, which is not a favourable context for what concerns innovative people management item (6), namely formative performance-enhanced appraisal. One interviewed mid-career professional says that, in spite of his eight-year experience in another industry as a middle-level manager, he had to start his new job from the lowest position, working as a simple operator in his first year, since the rigid human resources policy of the company that he joined has no fast-track advancement system. This also implies that he probably needs to wait for ten years, just like a fresh graduate, to be promoted and become a middle-level manager. Itami (2019) raises concern over the lack of big thinking in leadership among Japanese firms, stuck in their old glorious traditions, which leaves much room for improvement in innovative people management in relation to item (1), namely innovation-oriented vision and culture as a corporate strategic orientation.

Figure 4 summarizes the successes and failures of Japanese management's underlying people centric innovation ecosystem, based on the knowledge-worker perspective of the strategic people management model (Zhang-Zhang et al., 2022). Many Japanese enterprises have been able to sustain their performance in a durable way in both social and ecological terms. In a dynamic environment, they sense, organize, capture, and renew their capabilities through knowledge and technology. If technology disrupts the existing paradigm, an old ecosystem may die and a new ecosystem may be born. Following technology upgrades and renewal, it is the knowledge embedded in knowledge workers that makes it possible to innovate, create value, and mobilize the ecosystem communities with multiple stakeholders. For instance, in Japan's highly dynamic postwar context, a large number of transformative leaders emerged that took the helm and created an innovative culture in their organizations, pushing both tacit

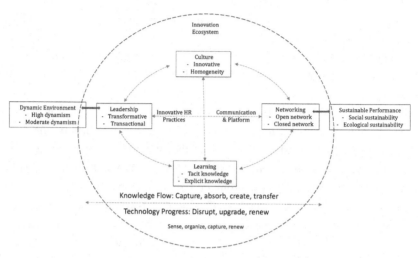

Figure 4 People centric innovation ecosystem

and explicit knowledge learning beyond organizational boundaries through collaborative networking. These innovative HR best practices, along with communication and platform, may evolve to be controversial when the environment is moderately dynamic. Transformative leadership becomes more transactional as the degree of professionalism grows. When the turbulence of the environment rises again, the system is unable to catch up unless it self-renews. A once successful network driven by innovation may also be too closed to align with today's digitized society.

Multiple Interactions of Innovation Ecosystems

Inoue's early description of Japanese-style management implicitly addresses the reflective learning of managers at the top and middle levels to configure their own theories, models, and systems to fit with the particularity of each company (Arnold, 1961). Based on these underlying knowledge and innovation hints, Ornatowski (1998) suggests that the innovative needs of large Japanese corporations require employees to release their creativity to generate market, product, and service innovation to compete in the global markets. Indeed, Japanese organizations have gradually recognized the need for a new style of people management to speedily and flexibly organize capabilities to compete internationally (Steffensen, 1998).

While some companies have risen or fallen, others have carried on and maintained their performance. For instance, the leading cloth retailer Uniqlo has pursued open innovation by collaborating with customers and external designers. Another example is Kyocera's Amoeba Management (Adler and Hiromoto, 2012; Inamori, 2013), with its unique organizational success that relies on splitting the community into small units functioning as independent ecosystems, meanwhile also interacting with other units and being interdependent. Thanks to extremely decentralized but strongly customer-focused independent amoebas, Kyocera keeps growing and maintains its high level of dynamism and employee commitment. Each small-sized amoeba, with five to 50 employees, is expected to devise its own plan and accounting system to collaborate with other amoebas and achieve profitable growth, supported with culture and incentive (Adler and Hiromoto, 2012). This decentralized model results in agile market responsiveness, high-quality customer service, employee empowerment, and a complete performance management system, compensating for the fact that fostering innovativeness is lacking in some traditional Japanese management practices (e.g., innovative people management items (6), (7), and (8)).

The Twelve Management Principles of Inamori's management philosophy start with the invitation to "clearly state the purpose and mission of your business," along with others like "keep passionate desire in your heart" and "always be creative in your work" (Kyocera, 2020). Market orientation, leadership development, and participating management are the three core components of Amoeba Management (Adler and Hiromoto, 2012). A leader's vision is the key element for dynamic strategic people management (Zhang et al., 2009; Zhang-Zhang, Rohlfer, and Varma, 2022), which directs the innovation strategy and culture as corporate strategic orientation to pursue item (1) of the innovative people management system. The proposed People Centric Innovation Ecosystem (Figure 4) is complemented by multidimensional interactions among ecosystems and their stakeholders in the communities, capable of self-renewal thanks to a more broadly defined innovative people centric management system (See Figure 5).

We can visualize the business world as multiple ecosystems (i.e., Ecosystem 1, 2, 3 ... n) that contain sub-ecosystems (i.e., Sub-ecosystem $1_1, 1_2, 1_3 ... 1_n$). These sub-ecosystems establish networks among them within their larger ecosystem and also interact with external ecosystems. All ecosystems are subject to the influence of the external environment, which is, in turn, affected by each ecosystem as well. Oriented by market, this vision of a business ecosystem mutually reinforces the knowledge interactions between the ecosystem and the market. In due course, ecosystems are also oriented toward stressing innovation performance for the sake of their sustainability and survival.

Besides these multiple relationships and interactions, the internal functioning of an ecosystem is people centric, as it relies on the humanistic approach to knowledge creation. Three dynamic people management elements form the core of the people centric management approach: leaders, innovative people

Figure 5 Multidimensional interactions of an innovation ecosystem

management and practices, and strategic learning. The vision of the leader sets the direction and the language of the ecosystem, its innovation-oriented strategy, and asupportive and developmental corporate culture. Strategic learning is the knowledge internalization that empowers the dynamic capability to sense, absorb, digest, reflect, and generate new knowledge and even ensure its later diffusion, while the nine innovative people management elements regulate daily practices for talent attraction, retention, motivation, and potential releasing.

6 Discussion and Learning for Asia's Emerging Powers

Although the Japanese economy has stagnated for decades, its long-standing productivity and innovative capabilities are still envied by many countries. What is more, Japan is the first country that emerged from the East and challenged the Western enterprises dominating global business, while also taking top rank as a developed economy in Asia. The rise, challenges, and enduring interest in Japanese management and its people centric innovation system deserve attention for the purpose of further discussion and learning that might benefit the global business communities and, especially, emerging enterprises in Asian countries.

The Contribution of Japanese Management

Over the past few decades, Japanese management practices have influenced management theory in general and, more specifically, the theoretical developments and practices of Western management, with Haghirian (2010) claiming that many Japanese management practices are standard in Western firms.

As Kotabe (2020) underlines, the contribution of Japanese management is not only discussed academically but also applied to the business reality, both in the Western context and in other Asian environments, regardless of the circumstances in which a firm operates and its corresponding management practices. Of the four areas in which Japanese management contributes to management theory (Westney, 2020), people/organizational behavior/organization studies and innovation/production/operation are the most frequently debated. Ogoshi (2006) argues that the Japanese wage system is still "person-oriented," even though the seniority-based wage system has been changed to performance- and ability-related rewards. The strategy area is also still strongly influenced by Nonaka's knowledge school of management. The conceptualization of the people centric innovation ecosystem sheds light on all three areas to integrate the contribution of Japanese management, offering the lesson that the soft factors, related to people/knowledge workers/human resources in the organization, and the hard factors should be combined (Nonaka and Johansson, 1985).

Still, according to Westney (2020), the fourth area to which Japanese management contributes is the field of international business, where we can observe the intertwined influence of American and Japanese approaches. Some classical Japanese management elements, like total quality management or just-in-time, were argued to be derived from learning and adoption of US practices. On the other hand, certain aspects regarded as pillars of Japanese management, including bottom-up processes, loyalty, commitment, and teamwork, were exported to the West to become an integral part of American management or general management and organization theory. Johnson and Ouchi's (1974) work not only addresses people-related management – like employees' well-being, managers at different levels, involvement in the decision-making process, communication, and information flow system – but also adds to the debate on the transferability of Japanese management into the American business context. Vice versa, when Japanese enterprises follow the American model of human resources management to transform themselves, it may become a kind of "Japan-style Americanization" (Ogoshi, 2006). Both the comparability and internationalization of Japanese firms operating in other countries and Western multinationals active in Japan have generated further interest and discussions on the particularity or generalizability of Japanese management or Western management/American management. As seen in Kase, Slocum, and Zhang's (2011) work on comparing Asian and Western management thinking, this is an area of potential investigation for future research. In the same vein, Makino and Lehmberg (2020) argue that the insights offered by Japanese management research can contribute to management theory in three ways, namely developing a theory of Japanese management, developing a Japanese theory of management, and developing a general theory of management from observation of Japanese experiences and practices in business and management.

Globalization and Japanese Management

The year 2022 was the thirtieth anniversary of International Federation of Scholarly Associations of Management's (IFSAM) first congress in Tokyo in 1992; the memory booklet describes numerous pieces of Western scholars' interests in Japan at that moment and Japanese scholars' interactions with the rest of the world (Castañer and Zhang-Zhang, 2022). Okubayashi (2022) particularly is concerned with the evolution of Japanese management and its interconnection with the rest of the world of management. Hasegawa (2006) debates the issue of transcendability from nationalistic management studies to global theoretical development. By listing the different initial studies on management in Britain, the United States, Germany, and France, Hasegawa traces the British predatory position back to 1776 in Adam Smith's *The Wealth of Nations*, underlining the late start of management studies in Japan as a capitalist nation, despite earlier commercial studies during the Edo (1603–1868) and Meji (1868–1912) periods. American theories of management and organization and German business economics had the greatest influence on Japanese managerial practices after World War II. Then, the growing overseas operations of Japanese enterprises drew attention to the analysis of different subsystems of the Japanese management system (Hayashi, 2002).

After the 1960s, the rise of this first Asian country broke the paradigm of Western dominance in the management discipline, which came to be viewed as characteristic of individual countries, corresponding to British, or American, or German, or Japanese management – or, more recently, Chinese management (Hasegawa, 2006). The national economic policy and underlying institutional factors largely influenced Japanese competitiveness in the energy industry, as well as in certain other industries and areas, with similarities and differences in their evolution patterns (Kikkawa, 2001). It is the international interest in Japan's global success that led to the theoretical development of Japanese-style management. The rise of a country's management studies, for example Japanese management, is from the practices and functional origin, even in a perspective of short-term actions (Hasegawa, 2006), which confirms the view of Japanese management evolution as being in accordance with the economic development (Kotabe, 2020) as described in Sections 2 and 3.

However, the enduring debate around Japanese management after the 1990s has largely concentrated on its transformation. This is considered critical to the survival of the theoretical transcendence of Japanese management and in terms of practical aspects affecting Japanese corporations, including not pursuing profit at the expense of their stakeholders (Hayashi, 2002), surviving and outcompeting, thanks to reformed management and practices, other global players from the West, as well as other Asian companies, for example Chinese and Korean. McCormick (2004) also points out that it is problematic to generalize how Japanese companies or management typically are in contemporary Japan, due to their complexity and different adaptations implemented in strategic decisions. McCormick gives the example of Toyota, one of the best-known prototypical Japanese companies, which is more likely to adapt to the local context at its international production sites than are rivals (e.g., Nissan and Honda). As discussed in Section 3, different types of Japanese enterprises may also have varied behaviors and strategic decision approaches.

Contextualization and Generalizability

Reflecting on Japanese management, Hasegawa (2006) also ponders whether management study is a social science. With inconsistencies between management theories and practices, business theories are often too contingent on multiple variables, including both internal and external factors. This implies a fundamental philosophical question as to what science is. Khun (2012) presents the structure of scientific evolutions with paradigm shifts, without distinguishing between natural sciences and social sciences. Risjord (2014) specifically discusses the distinctive nature of social sciences from a philosophical perspective. Ghoshal (2005) is more critical when it comes to determining whether the management field belongs to the social sciences and classes it, along with the aesthetic fields (e.g., arts), among the humanities. One of the differences between social sciences and natural sciences is that the former provides intentional explanations while the approach of the latter relies on causal explanation. From a different angle, Hasegawa (2006) views the US approach as functional but European management as more of a social science in nature since management studies incorporate social relation elements, like human issues. On the other hand, the supposedly "scientific approach" of the "profit-pursuit paradigm," based on functional elements, lacks aspects like sustainable development, social concerns, and a long-term view.

Another major difference between social sciences and natural sciences is the foundation of humanities in the former, which makes humans matter, given human intentionality. Conversely, the causal explanation and functional explanation modes entail dehumanization and their practices are questionable, among other issues (Ghoshal, 2005). Thus, the contradictory functional approach and ethical value-humanistic approach to management studies have caused a rift not only in management research as a discipline but also in business practices through management education. Hasegawa (2006) concludes that the first approach justifies unethical managerial behavior under the name of science, without leaving room for human ethics in the dynamic development paradigm of sustainable management. Adopting a more American management style in large Japanese enterprises causes Japanese employees to be more efficiency-oriented but, at the same time, to bear higher levels of stress for the sake of competitiveness. Under the profit-pursuit competitive paradigm, numerous cases of death or suicide from overwork (*karoshi*), as well as other labor, business, and financial scandals, have occurred not only in Japan (Hasegawa, 2006; Ogoshi, 2006) but also in Western countries and emerging economies like China.

Educated managers who believe in dehumanized managerial theories take them into action and practices and approach a purely profitability-maximizing paradigm, which leads to Ghoshal (2005: p. 87) claiming: "Excessive truth-claims based on extreme assumptions and partial analysis of complex phenomena can be bad even when they are not altogether wrong." On the one hand, the knowledge spiral embedded in business and management may accelerate the process of decreasing the effectiveness of certain once-successful management theories by creating nonheterogeneity in the analytical tools used to differentiate them from others. On the other hand, management theories generated in a specific geographical area need further testing in a variety of contexts before their generalizability can be ascertained. In sum, the universality of management theories is still being debated for what concerns its contextualization in terms of both temporal and geographical dimensions.

The creation of Responsible Research for Business and Management (RRBM) as a community aims to contribute research efforts in the management field to add sustainable value to society. Indeed, the principles of RRBM are service to society, valuing both basic and applied contributions, valuing plurality and multidisciplinary collaborations, sound methodology, stakeholder involvement, impact on stakeholders, and broad dissemination (RRBM, 2017). Ethics is not only a relevant feature for organizations so that people can become the foundation of their sustainable management, but it is also necessary for management scholars to be aware of and reflect on the purposes, processes, and potential consequences of their research. Hasegawa (2006) detects the irony that the superpowers' economic prowess may make them fail to look after human dignity due to corporate ideology, while economically less central countries may better preserve human dignity.

Japan is reported to have many old businesses, namely 33,000 businesses with at least 100 years of history and over 140 with more than 500 years, according to the Research Institute of Centennial Management (Dooley and Ueno, 2020). These long-lasting enterprises may be small, like traditional food retailers, or large, like Nintendo, and they have survived wars, natural disasters, and all kinds of institutional ups and downs by being less concerned about finances and choosing stability over profit (Dooley and Ueno, 2020). The oldest businesses in Japan have lasted for so long because they have adjusted to changing times (Nakazawa, 2020). Could this sustainable performance of Japanese enterprises with people centricity be generalizable to other settings, or is it only limited to the particular context of Japan? When Zhang-Zhang, Rohlfer, and Varma (2022) adopt a knowledge-worker perspective to examine strategic people management in highly dynamic VUCA contexts, they also argue in favor of applying to other situations the SECI model, developed in the Japanese context (Nonaka and Takeuchi, 1995). Kase, Slocum, and Zhang (2011) also suggest the inclusion of differential elements in the corresponding Asian versus Western management thinking. A similar analogy is valid in multiple theoretical generation processes, subject to the durability of their intentional explanatory power in both temporal and geographic contexts.

Culture and Metaculture Sources

One of the premises for a discussion around the particularity or generalizability of (Japanese) management theory is the country boundary limit. Defined either as Japanese theory of management or Japanese management theory, the existing literature has largely agreed that one of its determining factors is its cultural foundation (not boundary), of course also considering other influential factors. The alternative reasoning could be Dunphy's (1987) argument, suggesting that the unique features of the Japanese economic and political environment affect business operations. From this viewpoint, it seems that social-structural reasons rather than cultural ones determine the management goals in Japan. Nevertheless, in a complexly defined culture, social relationships are tied and interwoven with cultural value formation and mutual influencing occurs. Therefore, we interchangeably use these terms in this section. As early as 1958, Abegglen identified traditional social relationships and values as the source of natural growth for Japanese management. Over the years, this connotation has continued explicitly or implicitly in most discussions on the matter.

People Centric Paradigm

Researchers often use their own countries' management style as a benchmark (McCormick, 2004), similar to what happens in cross-cultural management when benchmarking against one's own culture. Earlier Japanese management theorists often attributed the dissimilarities between Japanese management and American management to behavioral differences in the two cultures, in a comparative fashion (e.g., Johnson and Ouchi, 1974). Some addressed cultural differences by looking at attitudes toward individualism versus collectivism, competitivism versus peopleism, specialist versus generalist, and their associated values. In view of the preceding discussion on contextualization and generalization, it can be said that certain management practices are not necessarily nationally bound, but transcendable to a general ethics-centric management paradigm as meta culture, as seen in Johnson and Ouchi's (1974) work highlighting Japanese management's intrinsic element of caring for people. Although American management has a more direct focus on organizational performance and intrinsic elements are of secondary importance, caring for people is still a relevant metacultural variable. The core issue has to do with different orders of priorities in diverse settings, in this case framed through the Japanese–American comparison.

Noda and Glazer (1968) discuss the need for American expatriates to be flexible in adapting to the cultural differences found in Japan. Similarly, Pascale (1978) states that difficulties in applying Japanese management techniques to a Western industrial system arise from personnel practices or cultural differences. Nonetheless, some of these cultural differences are superficial, merely behavioral reflections of the underlying cultural value system, subject to the relatively easy changes and evolution occurring in society and mutual awareness over time. Culture is a dynamic element that may evolve in society to bring about cultural differences across generations, while also affecting other levels of culture, for example industrial, professional, and regional (Rohlfer and Zhang, 2016). Cultural configuration is much more complex than the simplified structure measured in most research contributions.

The intrinsic interests in caring for people in Japanese management not only provide stable employment relations, but also found the common-good approach of managing people, as Aust, Matthews and Muller-Camen (2020) propose. In pursuit of sustainable development, management scholars around the world have been advocating a paradigmatic shift from the "economic man" to a humanistic approach. The deeply rooted people centric value in Japanese management, with a people management perspective based on the common good, may deserve more attention and represent a source of learning for others, in spite of its own embedded challenges and self-evolution.

Innovation Ecosystem Paradigm

According to Howard and Teramoto (1981), the Japanese philosophy incorporated the imported Confucianist/Taoist framework of complementarity, which enables the existence of a multisystem, or multiple ecosystems, which may be viewed as chaotic and irrational by Westerners. For example, the concept of *ie* (family) reflects the cultural root in Japanese management for a paternalistic system that loosely restricts the Japanese family system in enterprises; *zaibatsu*, management of family members, adds the way to manage employees in an *ie* concept (Noda and Glazer, 1968). Within loosely networked ecosystems, people are the core elements and foundation of *ie*, as Kumagai (1992) says when describing the *kanji* (Chinese character) for *ie*.

Within a family contextualization, business is viewed in Japan as a community whose members share a common fate rather than simply as a means to maximize the rate of return on investment (Howard and Teramoto, 1981). Organic harmony and a dualistic/ paradoxical vision are also part of Japanese management's cultural underpinnings (Yang, 1984), derived from the Taoist philosophy. With its holistic and long-term vision, the *ie* family system is based on the trust of family members, or in-group members, which reduces the cost and level of difficulty of negotiations among the community members within the ecosystem, eventually accelerating technological innovation processes. Examples of this include Toyota and Hitachi, which have formed business ecosystems composed of subcontractors, merchandising organizations, and banks, among other stakeholders (Howard and Teramoto, 1981). On the other hand, in a collective family organizational cultural context, it is difficult for individuals to explicitly distinguish their performance from that of the group; also, in order not to highlight their individual performance, members may not dare to significantly contribute to the *ringi* decision-making process as its spirit calls for (Yang, 1984).

Recognized as demand-pull and customer-oriented, Japanese enterprises seem to have a superior probability of achieving market success, despite performing better in an incremental innovation context (Gerstenfeld and Sumiyoshi, 1980). In a 2021 interview, a senior international manager that had been living and working in Tokyo for more than twenty years commented that the Japanese are extremely innovative and take care of every single detail in their daily tasks; salespersons often have creative ideas to find the most appropriate solution for their clients. In a business context, innovation is a wide concept going beyond technology and more closely related to successful commercialization of new products and their market adoption, and even management innovation. Innovating into the details of process is another illustration that shows the success of Japanese management, intertwining the interests of stakeholders (i.e. customer and enterprises in this case) in the innovation ecosystem. An integrative view of the customer as part of the business ecosystem of the enterprises rather than a win-lose position enables innovative initiatives, which seem to be key to sustainable development in Japanese enterprises as an ecosystematic approach, as suggested by Zhang-Zhang, Rohlfer, and Rajasekera (2020).

Coexistence of Convergence and Divergence

As early as 1987, Dunphy (1987: p. 445) contributed to the discussion on the convergence/ divergence of Japanese and Western enterprises and management, initiated by Veblen's argument that the two would converge as countries modernized: "organizational structures and value systems inevitably converge." In detail, most writings before the 1970s favored the convergence theory and saw Japanese management as an obstacle to the advancement of a universal management theory or even to economic progress. These Japanese challenges or disturbances bothered some Western researchers, since they were contrary to what were regarded as the principles of management in the Western world, particularly in the United States (Yoshino, 1968).

Though either convergence or divergence prevailed in different periods of time during the evolution of Japanese management, we can observe that neither approach gained complete dominance. Rather, there have been changes in the overall tendency, sometimes even artificially created by academics. For example, a convergence approach regarding Japanese management initially took hold among Western commentators, but there were also alternative opinions on the persistence of Japanese management's unique features (Ballon, 1969), like *nenko*, the traditional seniority-based remuneration system. Later, when the divergence approach prevailed, Japanese management was recognized among international scholars as a separate paradigm, differentiated from the Western one. It is in this period that Western management learned from the Japanese context and adopted some of its practices. But, at the time of the economic downturn, the transformation of Japanese enterprises and their HRM practices caused an even stronger convergence (Frenkel, 1994; Ornatowski, 1998). However, this process could also be viewed as self-evolution, meaning that some Japanese management practices were retained while others were abandoned (Dunphy, 1987). Indeed, an innovative ecosystem implies the ability to self-transform, which, in our case, enables the community members to generate new Japanese management, absorbing good practices from American management (Kuroda, 2006; Ogoshi, 2006) instead of striving for convergence.

The debate around convergence or divergence is most often tackled from an American perspective. On the one hand, what is Western management? Pudelko (2004) studied mutual learning between Japanese and Western HRM (i.e., American and German) and found that, although Japanese HR managers mainly looked to American management, they also perceived that a more balanced model, like the German one, may offer valuable guidance, with a better fit in the Japanese context. Despite the fact that German and American management are forms of Western management, they also differ from each other. Is the Japanese model converging toward the Western model, or indeed the American one? Both earlier literature and Pudelko (2004) show that it is a mutual learning process, though one may adopt more from the other at certain times, rather than a unidirectional process taking the American system as a benchmark, with Japan as the only nation converging or diverging from the ethnocentric American view. That is to say, during the period when American enterprises adopted Japanese management and practices, why was the phenomenon not referred to as convergence to the Japanese management system?

From a linear Western viewpoint, things need to move in one direction or another, namely "either/or," and one inevitably needs to choose convergence or divergence when looking at Japanese and Western management. However, in a holistic Asian view, the world can accommodate the coexistence of "both/ and," a notion derived from the Taoist philosophy, which allows the two trends to inclusively co-occur, as Rohlfer and Zhang (2016) state in relation to paradigmatic shifts in cultural studies on international business – a coexistence of convergence and divergence.

Discussion

While arguing for a people centric innovation ecosystem based on Japanese management and practices, we praise the people-oriented values in Japanese organizations, but also criticize its traditionalism, very much in need of transformation. We praise the innovative capability of its community and ecosystem view, but also criticize its having a relatively closed ecosystem instead of an open platform. While Japanese enterprises have been largely successful in an industrialization era with incremental innovations, improving precision and efficiency, digitalization may require more disruptive innovation, including business model innovation across sectors and new ecosystem building. Digitalization has been a tech trend and innovation source for business and management from the beginning of the twenty-first century. Diversity and inclusion have also been called for to achieve the sustainable development of society. A relatively homogeneous society, with a clear family-labor division structure, had an effective role in the earlier period of Japan's rapid industrialization and economic development. However, it may be a hindrance in a digital paradigm whose open structure requires diverse inputs for innovation. The following paragraphs discuss the role of women in this diversity play, but diversity is crucial also in terms of international profiles and other dimensions in the workforce. We then conclude by discussing some implications for Asia's emerging markets.

Womenomics and Women in the Workplace

As for employment relationships in Japan, a topic that is crucial but not widely discussed within the Japanese management context is gender equality and women's participation and leadership in the workforce. Japan's population decrease and aging society require more women to join the labor market to fill the labor gap and support stable economic development. The determined "womenomics" policy of the former Japanese Prime Minister Shinzo Abe to make women shine did not reach the expected goals, even though progress was made (Oda and Reynolds 2018). Among the OECD countries, Japan also has quite a low ranking in what concerns the Global Gender Gap. The resignation of the president of the Tokyo Olympics committee, due to his gender-discriminating remarks, reflects the country's reality in relation to gender equality (Harding, 2021).

As mentioned in Section 2, some early literature placed women's labor in the same category as part-time and temporary work and, traditionally, this was indeed the main role of women in the Japanese labor market. Though times have changed and females are playing a more relevant role in Japanese economic development and organizations, they are still under-represented in many fields, for example as legislators, senior officials, and managers. Women's employment rate is comparable with that of European countries and has been improving, but 57.7 percent of women are engaged in nonregular employment (Reality Check Team, 2018).

Some young female interviewees compared the number of women managers in their organizations in Japan and in Chinese subsidiaries, concluding that in China women are more equally treated as regards career opportunities. However, in another interview conducted in 2019 with Ms. Ogushi, former president of the FujiXerox Learning Institute, she stated that she did not perceive any discrimination against women in her organization. Yet, she also added that this was probably due to the knowledge-intensive industry in which she worked. Indeed, gender inequality might be greater in heavy industries and, overall, it is difficult to make broad generalizations. Zhang-Zhang and Kumagai (2020) identify several contributing factors to the phenomenon, among which are issues regarding society and traditions, like parents' gender differentiation in education; social pressure, like long working hours and out-of-office drinking culture in Japanese corporations; relatively weak legal protection, although the Equal Employment Opportunity Law (EEOL) was enacted in 1986; an average pay gap of 24.5 percent; and other general aspects, including career opportunities and motivation, as well as corporate culture.

The issue of gender in Japan is not only a matter of expanding the potential workforce to make up for labor shortages, but it also has to do with bringing diversified profiles into the workplace to spark innovation. In 2021, the New York Stock Market and Germany, among others, set explicit quotas for female members in the boards of directors of publicly listed large corporations, and Japanese enterprises may need similar actions to attain a diversified talent pool in terms of not only gender but also internationality.

Implications for Asian Emerging Economies

As remarked by Spender (2014), quoting the words of a student in a talk, "academics sometimes try to do with their heads what they cannot do with their hearts (or guts)." Indeed, rationalizing and putting things into a logical formula seems to be the job of an academic. The proposed people centric innovation ecosystem may well be just another attempt at using academic language to construct nothing truly new in the real world. As a means of expression, however, language constructs might interpret a set of circumstances from different angles, which may offer a different perspective (Spender, 2021).

The rise, fall, stagnation, and recovery of Japan's economy and management provide a lesson for the world, especially for the Asian emerging economy context. Although Japan has not fully regained its competitive position in IMD's World Competitiveness Ranking since it started in 1989 (Makino and Lehmberg, 2020), the evolution path of its management and its sustainability in many essential dimensions could be benchmarked as a development with similarities to that of emerging powers in the East.

Today's business world is looking at China's emerging productivity and management. In Section 2, we reported web search data on Japanese management and we did similar searches on February 8, 2021 about European management (4,850,000 results), Chinese management (around 4,500,000 results), and American management (4,320,000 results). These numbers are significantly higher than the 3,780,000 results for Japanese management, albeit without large differences. Despite growing interest in Chinese management, there is no clear innovative academic conceptualization, like Theory Z or the Knowledge-Creating Company theory, to establish a knowledge school of thought in organization and profoundly impact the worldwide academia. The *Guanxi* or *Ying-Yang* theories have been popular in recent decades but they are informative, striving to provide explanatory value, rather than being truly transformative for the management field.

A competitive dynamism perspective may be one of the best attempts at conceptualization in the field of strategy.

Like Japan in the 1950s, focusing on upgrading the quality of its products to reverse the negative connotation of "Made in Japan" goods (Keys and Miller, 1984), China has been making similar efforts to upgrade its innovation capabilities. Its general innovation competence has been enhanced, but the negative connotations attached to "Made in China" products are still to be eliminated. The same can be said about the country's image as regards innovation and management when dealing with internationalization (Zhang and Zhou, 2015). Because it shares certain similarities in cultural background, especially in comparison with Western management, the Japanese management and path may provide valuable lessons for Chinese management and that of other Asian nations, such as Indonesia, India, or Vietnam, in spite of the differences pointed out by some between Japanese enterprises and those located elsewhere in Asia.

As the first non-Western country that joined the group of highly industrialized powers, sometimes Japan has been included among the Western economies. The success of its management during periods of economic boom was because Japanese management and practices fitted the needs of the economic, cultural, legal, and technological environment of that time (Kotabe, 2020). Chinese management and other Asian management types may benefit from this contextualization, with both temporal and geographical dimensions, in creating their own management style or in pursuing extension to a more general management theory, so that ethics and humans are placed at the center of attention. Although the current digitalization is a new phenomenon, differentiating the present from the 1970s and 1980s, the emerging economy period retains similar characteristics for the most part. We do not advocate applying traditional Japanese management to the emerging Asian economies as a reference point to benchmark, but it might be worthwhile to benchmark Japan's development process and people centric, innovative ecosystem as the core philosophy and principle of a development path.

It is also highly probable that the Japanese management style, as described in different studies, and the people centric innovation ecosystem work well in the entrepreneurial stage of business introduction and growth. When Japanese economy emerged, it was characterized by entrepreneurial spirits to expand to American and other occidental worlds. In such a business scenario, uncertainty and unclear rules (ambiguity) are the norm and continuous discussions, debates, and challenges are needed to find the optimal solution for the context given. This may not apply in a relatively mature context, in which dynamism is greatly reduced and there is an established set of patterns of external and internal behavior, not considering potential sudden disruptions, like crises (volatility), calling for a dramatic transformation. The latter could be caused by both internal and external disruptive innovations or unforeseen forces, like COVID-19. The complexity of this highly dynamic VUCA environment demands an innovative ecosystem view for business management in this shifting paradigm, with people at the center to govern knowledge management.

References

Abegglen, J. C. (1958). *The Japanese Factory: Aspects of Its Social Organization*. Glencoe, IL: Free Press.

Adler, R. W., and Hiromoto, T. (2012). Amoeba management: Lessons from Japan's Kyocera. *MIT Sloan Management Review*, 54(1), 83–89.

Adner, R. (2006). Match your innovation strategy to your innovation ecosystem. *Harvard Business Review*, 84(4), 98–107.

Adner, R., and Kapoor, R. (2010). Value creation in innovation ecosystems: How the structure of technological interdependence affects firm performance in new technology generations. *Strategic Management Journal*, 31(3), 306–333.

Aonuma, Y. (1965). *Nihon no Keieiso* [*The Managerial Class in Japan*]. Tokyo: NihonKeizai Shinbun Sha.

Arnold, W. J. (1961). Japanese management rates itself: An experiment in appraising business efficiencies. *Academy of Management Journal*, 4(2), 144–148.

Arora, A., Belenzon, S., and Patacconi, A. (2019). A theory of the US innovation ecosystem: Evolution and the social value of diversity. *Industrial and Corporate Change*, 28(2), 289–307.

Aust, I., Matthews, B., and Muller-Camen, M. (2020). Common good HRM: A paradigm shift in sustainable HRM? *Human Resource Management Review*, 30(3), 100705.

Avex Marketing Inc. (2013). WhiteFlame (official website). Accessed on December 14, 2020, at avex.jp/whiteflame/index.html.

Bacon, E., Williams, M. D., and Davies, G. (2020). Coopetition in innovation ecosystems: A comparative analysis of knowledge transfer configurations. *Journal of Business Research*, 115, 307–316. https://doi.org/10.1016/j .jbusres.2019.11.005

Ballon, R. J. (1969). Lifelong remuneration system. In R. J. Ballon, ed., *The Japanese Employee*. Tokyo: Sophia University Press, pp. 123–165.

Ballon, R. J. (1983). Non-Western work organizations. *Asia Pacific Journal of Management*, 1, 1–14.

Basole, R. C., and Karla, J. (2011). On the evolution of mobile platform ecosystem structure and strategy. *Business and Information Systems Engineering*, 3(5), 313–322.

Bassis, N. F., and Armellini, F. (2018). Systems of innovation and innovation ecosystems: A literature review in search of complementarities. *Journal of*

Evolutionary Economics, 28, 1053–1080. https://doi.org/10.1007/s00191-018-0600-6

Bhappu, A. D. (2000). The Japanese family: An institutional logic for Japanese corporate networks and Japanese management. *Academy of Management Review*, 25(2), 409–415.

Bloom, S. (1982). *Video Invaders*. New York: Arco Publishing.

Buckley, P. J., and Mirza, H. (1985). The wit and wisdom of Japanese management: An iconoclastic analysis. *Management International Review*, 25(3), 16–32.

Castañer, X., and Zhang-Zhang, Y. (eds.) (2022). *Memory Booklet of 1992 IFSAM Tokyo Congress*. Brussels: International Federation of Scholarly Associations of Management.

Cavusgil, S. T., Ghauri, P. N., and Akcal, A. A. (2013). *Doing Business in Emerging Markets*, 2nd ed. London: SAGE.

Chae, B. K. (2019). A general framework for studying the evolution of the digital innovation ecosystem: The case of big data. *International Journal of Information Management*, 45, 83–94. https://doi.org/10.1016/j.ijinfomgt.2018.10.023

Chesbrough, H., Kim, S., and Agogino, A. (2014). Chez Panisse: Building an open innovation ecosystem. *California Management Review*, 56(4), 144–171.

Collinson, S., and Rugman, A. M. (2008). The regional nature of Japanese multinational business. *Journal of International Business Studies*, 39(2), 215–230.

Craig, T. (2020). *"Kawaii": Hello Kitty and Japanese Cute, Cool Japan*. Broadway, NY: Blue Sky Publishing.

Crypton Future Media (2020). *Character Usage Guidelines*. Accessed on December 14, 2020, at https://piapro.jp/license/character_guideline (in Japanese).

Dabney, T. (2016). *Forward 1, in Herman, L. Phoenix IV: The History of the Videogame Industry*, 4th ed. Springfield, NJ: Rolenta Press.

de Vasconcelos Gomes, L. A., Figueiredo Facin, A. L., Salerno, M. S., and Ikenami, R. K. (2018). Unpacking the innovation ecosystem construct: Evolution, haps and trends. *Technological Forecasting and Social Change*, 136(4), 30–48.

Dooley, B., and Ueno, H. (2020). This Japanese shop is 1,020 years old. It knows a bit about surviving crises. *The New York Times*, December 2. Accessed on December 9, 2020, at www.nytimes.com/2020/12/02/business/japan-old-companies.html?algo=als1.

Drucker, P. F. (1971). What we can learn from Japanese management. *Harvard Business Review*, 49 (2), 110–122.

Drucker, P. (1993). *Post-Capitalist Society*. London: Butterworth Heinemann.

Dunphy, D. (1987). Convergence divergence: A temporal review of the Japanese enterprise and its management. *Academy of Management Review*, 12(3), 445–459.

Endo, T., Delbridge, R., and Morris, J. (2015). Does Japan still matter? Past tendencies and future opportunities in the study of Japanese firms. *International Journal of Management Reviews*, 17(1), 101–123.

England, G. W., and Lee, R. (1971). Organizational goals and expected behavior among American, Japanese and Korean managers: Comparative study. *Academy of Management Journal*, 14(4), 425–438.

England, G. W., and Lee, R. (1974). Relationship between managerial values and managerial success in the United States, Japan, India, and Australia. *Journal of Applied Psychology*, 59(4), 411–419.

Fagerberg, J., Fosaas, M., and Sapprasert, K. (2012). Innovation: Exploring the knowledge base. *Research Policy*, 41(7), 1132–1153.

Fitzgerald, R., and Rowley, C. (2015). How have Japanese multinational companies changed? Competitiveness, management and subsidiaries. *Asia Pacific Business Review*, 21(3), 449–456.

Freeman, C. (1987). *Technology, Policy, and Economic Performance: Lessons from Japan*. London: Pinter Publishers.

Frenkel, S. (1994). Patterns of workplace relations in the global corporation: Toward convergence? In J. Belanger, P. K. Edwards, and L. Haiven, eds., *Workplace Industrial Relations and the Global Challenge*. Ithaca, NY: Cornell University Press, pp. 210–274.

Froomkin, J. N. (1964). Management and organization in Japanese industry. *Academy of Management Journal*, 7(1), 71–76.

Fujita, T., and Karger, D. (1972). Managing R and D in Japan. *Management International Review*, 12(1), 65–82.

Fukuda, K., and Watanabe, C. (2008). Japanese and US perspectives on the National Innovation Ecosystem. *Technology in Society*, 30(1), 49–63.

Furusawa, M., Brewster, C., and Takashina, T. (2016). Normative and systems integration in human resource management in Japanese multinational companies. *Multinational Business Review*, 24(2), 82–105.

Gawer, A. (2014). Bridging differing perspectives on technological platforms: Toward an integrative framework. *Research Policy*, 43(7), 1239–1249.

Gawer, A., and Cusumano, M. A. (2008). How companies become platform leaders. *MIT Sloan Management Review*, 49(2), 28–35.

Gerdeman, D. (2020). Why Japanese businesses are so good at surviving crises. *Harvard Business School Working Knowledge*, June 26, 2020. https://hbswk .hbs.edu/item/why-japan-s-businesses-are-so-good-at-surviving-crises?

cid=spmailing-33454779-WK%20Newsletter%206–23-2021%20(1)-June%
2023,%202021.

Gerlach, M. L. (1992). The Japanese corporate network: A blockmodel analysis. *Administrative Science Quarterly*, 37, 105–139.

Gerstenfeld, A., and Sumiyoshi, K. (1980). Management of innovation in Japan: Seven forces that make the difference. *Research Management*, 23 (1), 30–34.

Ghoshal, S. (2005). Bad management theories are destroying good management practices. *Academy of Management Learning & Education*, 4(1), 75–91.

Girotra, K., and Netessine, S. (2014). Four paths to business model innovation. *Harvard Business Review*, 92, 96–103.

Givens, S. (2022). Sony's lack of ecosystem poses an existential threat. *Nikkei Asia*, January 21, 2022. Accessed on February 7, 2022, at https://asia .nikkei.com/Opinion/Sony-s-lack-of-ecosystem-poses-an-existential-threat.

Gobble, M. M. (2014). Charting the innovation ecosystem. *Research Technology Management*, 57(4), 55–59.

Grant, R. M. (2013). Nonaka's "Dynamic Theory of Knowledge Creation" (1994): Reflections and an exploration of the "Ontological Dimension." In G. von Krogh, K. Kase, and C. Canton, eds., *Towards an Organizational Theory*. Basingstoke: Palgrave Macmillan, pp. 77–95.

Grant, R. M. (2016). *Contemporary Strategy Analysis*, 9th ed. Hoboken, NJ: Wiley.

Guerrero, M., and Martínez-Chávez, M. (2020). Aligning regional and business strategies: Looking inside the Basque Country entrepreneurial innovation ecosystem. *Thunderbird International Business Review*, 62(5), 607–621.

Guillén, M. (2001). *The Limits of Convergence: Globalization and Organizational Change in Argentina, South Korea, and Spain*. Princeton, NJ: Princeton University Press.

Haghirian, P. (2010). *Understanding Japanese Management Practices*. New York: Business Expert Press.

Harding, R. (2021). Tokyo Olympic boss's resignation fuels Japan gender equality debate. *Financial Times*. February 15. Accessed on February 18, 2021, at www.ft.com/content/0fb1b205-75a1-43b3-a056-d4996b580a74.

Hasegawa, H. (2006). Developing management studies as a social science: Globalization and Japanese management studies. *Asian Business & Management*, 5, 67–85.

Hatayama, K., and Kubo, M. (2000). *Pokémon Story*. Japan: Nikkei BP.

Hatvany, N., and Pucik, V. (1981). An integrated management system: Lessons from the Japanese experience. *Academy of Management Review*, 6(3), 469–480.

Hayashi, K. (1978a). Japanese management of multinational operations: Sources and means of control. *Management International Review*, 18(4), 47–57.

Hayashi, K. (1978b). Corporate planning practices in Japanese multinationals. *Academy of Management Journal*, 21(2), 211–226.

Hayashi, M. (2002). A historical review of Japanese management theories: The search for a general theory of Japanese management. *Asian Business & Management*, 1, 189–207.

Herman, L. (2016). *Phoenix IV: The History of the Videogame Industry*, 4th ed., Springfield, NJ: Rolenta Press.

Herz, J. C. (1997). *Joystick Nation*. Boston, MA: Little, Brown and Company.

Hirasaka, M., Kusaka, Y., and Brogan, J. (2021). Japanese style management in eras of change: New management model. *SN Business & Economics* 1(85), 1–18.

Horn, S. A., and Cross, A. R. (2009). Japanese management at a crossroads? The changing role of China in the transformation of corporate Japan. *Asia Pacific Business Review*, 15(3), 285–308.

Howard, N., and Teramoto, Y. (1981). The really important difference between Japanese and Western management. *Management International Review*, 21 (3), 19–30.

Huang, H., Chen, J., Yu, F., and Zhu, Z. (2019). Establishing the enterprises' innovation ecosystem based on dynamics core competence – The case of China's high-speed railway. *Emerging Markets Finance & Trade*, 55, 843–862. https://doi.org/10.1080/1540496X.2018.1518216

Hwang, V. (2014). The next big business buzzword: Ecosystem? *Forbes*, April 16. forbes.com/sites/victorhwang/2014/04/16/the-next-big-businessbuzzword-ecosystem.

Iansiti, M., and Levien, R. (2004). *The Keystone Advantage: What the New Dynamics of Business Ecosystems Mean for Strategy, Innovation, and Sustainability*. Boston, MA: Harvard Business School Press.

Inamori, K. (2013). *Amoeba Management*. Boca Raton, FL: CRC Press.

Independent Investigation Commission on the Fukushima Daiichi Nuclear Accident. (2012). *Investigation and Verification Report* 福島原発事故独立検証委員会, 調査・検証報告書, Tokyo: Discover; Rebuild Japan Initiative Foundation. (In Japanese.)

Independent Investigation Commission on the Fukushima Daiichi Nuclear Accident. (2014). *The Fukushima Daiichi Nuclear Power Station Disaster: Investigating the Myth and Reality*. Edited by M. K. Bricker. London and New York: Routledge.

Itami, H. (2019). Thinking big. In Itami, H., *Peoplism*, Chapter 6, teaching note on Development of Japanese Industries and Innovation. Minamiuonuma City: International University of Japan.

Itami, H., and Roehl, T. (1987). *Mobilizing Invisible Assets*. Cambridge: Harvard University Press.

Jacoby, S. M. (2005). *The Embedded Corporation: Corporate Governance and Employee Relations in Japan and the United States*. Princeton, NJ: Princeton University Press.

Jacoby, S. M. (2012). Forward. In Sakikawa, T., *Transforming Japanese Workplaces*. London: Palgrave MacMillan, pp. x–xiv.

Jiang, H., Gao, S., Zhao, S., and Cheng, H. (2020). Competition of technology standards in Industry 4.0: An innovation ecosystem perspective. *Systems Research and Behavioral Science*, 37(4), 772–783.

Johnson, R. T., and Ouchi, W. G. (1974). Made in America (under Japanese management). *Harvard Business Review*, 52(5), 61–69.

Jones, K. (2020). *Online Gaming: The Rise of a Multi-Billion Dollar Industry*, July 15, 2020. www.visualcapitalist.com/online-gaming-the-rise-of-a-multi-billion-dollar-industry/.

Kagono, T., Nonaka, I., Sakakibara, K., and Okumura, A. (1985). *Strategic vs. Evolutionary Management: A U.S.-Japan Comparison of Strategy and Organization*. Amsterdam: North-Holland.

Kaplan, S., and Lerner, J. (2010). It ain't broke: The past, present, and future of venture capital. *Journal of Applied Corporate Finance*, 22(2), 36–47.

Kase, K., Canton, C. G., and Zhang, Y. (2012). Fukushima Daiichi Nuclear Power Station (NPS). Teaching Note, May, IES270, IESE Business School Case Publishing.

Kase, K., Choi, E., and Nonaka, I. (2022). *Dr Kazuo Inamori's Management Praxis and Philosophy: A Response to the Profit-Maximisation Paradigm*. London: Palgrave MacMillan.

Kase, K., Nonaka, I., and Independent Panel (2012). *Fukushima Daiichi Nuclear Power Station (NPS)*. May, IES269, IESE Business School Case Publishing.

Kase, K., Slocum, A., and Zhang, Y. (2011). *Asian versus Western Management Thinking: Its Culture-Bound Nature*. Basingstoke: Palgrave MacMillan.

Kelley, L., and Reeser, C. (1973). Persistence of culture as a determinant of differentiated attitudes on part of American managers of Japanese ancestry. *Academy of Management Journal*, 16(1), 67–76.

Kent, S. L. (2010). *The Ultimate History of Video Games: From Pong to Pokémon and Beyond – The Story Behind the Craze that Touched our Lives and Changed the World*. New York: Three Rivers Press.

Kerr, A. (2001). *Dogs and Demons: The Fall of Modern Japan*. London: Penguin Books.

Keys, J. B., and Miller, T. R. (1984). The Japanese management theory jungle. *Academy of Management Review*, 9(2), 342–353.

Keys, J. B., Denton, L. T., and Miller, T. R. (1994). The Japanese management theory jungle – revisited. *Journal of Management* 20(2), 373–402.

Kikkawa, T. (1995a). *Kigyo Shudan*: The formation and functions of enterprise groups. *Business History* 37(2), 44–53.

Kikkawa, T. (1995b). The Japanese corporate system and economic growth. In Vol. XXXVII of *Annals of The Institute of Social Science*. Tokyo: The University of Tokyo Press, pp. 21–50.

Kikkawa, T. (2001). The government-industry relationship in Japan: What the history of the electric power industry teaches us. In Arne Holzhausen, ed., *Can Japan Globalize?* Heidelberg: Physica-Verlag, pp. 21–34.

Kikkawa, T. (2004). Japanese corporations in the 1990s: The end of the "Japanese Style" management? In G. Foljanty-Jost, ed., *Japan in the 1990s: Crisis as an Impetus for Change*. Münster, Germany: LIT Verlag, pp. 55–75.

Kikkawa, T. (2005). Toward the rebirth of the Japanese economy and its corporate system. *Japan Forum*, 17(1), 87–106.

Kikkawa, T. (2007). Economic growth and Japanese business management. In M. Miyamoto, T. Abe, M. Udagawa, M. Sawai, and T. Kikkawa, eds., *The Business History of Japan*. Tokyo: Yuhikaku Publishing.

Kikkawa, T. (2014). Nihonteki Keiei to sono Henyou (Japanese-style management and its transfomation). In M. Miyamoto, K. Okabe, and K. Hirano (Ed.). *1 kara no Keieishi* (The 1st step of business history). Sekigakusha, pp. 281–298.

Kikkawa, T. (2019). *Inobeshon no Rekishi (History of Innovations)*. Tokyo: Yuhikaku Publishing.

Kimberly, J. R., and Evanisko, M. J. (1981). Organizational innovation: The influence of individual, organizational, and contextual factors on hospital adoption of technological and administrative innovations. *The Academy of Management Journal*, 24(4), 689–713.

Kishi, M. (2003). Foreign direct investment by Japanese firms and corporate governance: In relation to the monetary policies of China, Korea and Japan. *Journal of Asian Economics*, 13(6), 731–748.

Kohler, C. (2016). *Power-up: How Japanese Video Games Gave the World an Extra Life*. New York: Dover Publications.

Kotabe, M. (2020). Japanese management and the climate of the time. *Asian Business & Management*, 19(1), 25–35.

Koyama, N. (2005). *The Power of Play: Namco's High Value-Added Strategy* 遊びのチカラ ナムコの高付加価値戦略. Japan: Nikkei BP Planning. (in Japanese)

Koyama, Y. (2013). HATSUNE Miku: User generated contents open the new world. *Systems, Control and Information*, 57(5), 183–188.

Kubota, A. (1982). Japanese employment system and Japanese social structure. *Asia Pacific Community*, 15(6), 96–120.

Kumagai, F. (1992). Research on the family in Japan. In UNESCO, ed., *The Changing Family in Asia: Bangladesh, India, Japan, Philippines, and Thailand*. Bangkok: UNESCO Principal Regional Office for Asia and the Pacific, pp. 159–237.

Kuniya, N., and L. Cooper Cary (1978). Participative management practice and work humanisation in Japan. *Personnel Review* 7(2), 25–30.

Kuroda, K. (2006). Japanese personnel management and flexibility today. *Asian Business & Management*, 5, 453–468.

Kvedaravičienė, G. (2019). Economic policy and open innovation ecosystems: Biomedicine case. *Organizacijų Vadyba: Sisteminiai Tyrimai*, 82(1), 53–69.

Kyocera (2020). What are the twelve management principles? Accessed on December 12, 2020, at https://global.kyocera.com/inamori/management/twelve/.

Kyodo (2022). Japan sees meter-high waves and tsunami warning after massive Tonga eruption. *The Japan Times*, January 16 2022. www.japantimes.co.jp/news/2022/01/16/national/japan-tsunami-tonga-volcano/.

Lee, Y., and Shin, J. (2018). Fintech: Ecosystem, business models, investment decisions, and challenges. *Business Horizon*, 61(1), 35–46.

Levine, S. B., and Kawada, S. B. (1980). *Human resources in Japanese industrial development*. Princeton, NJ: Princeton University Press.

Liu, E., and Zhang, Y. (2014). Learning process and capability formation in cross-border buyer-supplier relationships: A qualitative case study of Taiwanese technological firms. *International Business Review*, 23(4), 718–730.

Lusch, R. F., Vargo, S. L., and Gustafsson, A. (2016). Fostering a trans-disciplinary perspective of service ecosystems. *Journal of Business Research*, 69(8), 2957–2963.

Makino, S., and Lehmberg, D. (2020). The past and future contributions of research on Japanese management. *Asian Business & Management*, 19(1), 1–7.

March, J. G. (2004). Parochialism in the evolution of a research community: The case of organization studies. *Management and Organization Review*, 1(1), 5–22.

Markides, C. (1997). Strategic innovation. *MIT Sloan Management Review*, 38 (spring), 9–23.

Martin, B. R. (2012). The evolution of science policy and innovation studies. *Research Policy*, 41, 1219–1239.

Maruta, Y. (1980). Management of innovation in Japan: Tetsuri way. *Research Management*, 23(1), 39–41.

Mayer, R. E. (1999). Fifty years of creativity research. In R. J. Sternberg, ed., *Handbook of Creativity*. London: Cambridge University Press, pp. 449–460.

McCormick, K. (2004). Whatever happened to "the Japanese Model"? *Asian Business & Management*, 3, 371–393.

Miyajima, R. (1986). Organization ideology of Japanese managers. *Management International Review* 26(1), 73–76.

Miyamoto, M. (1996). The management systems of Edo Period Merchant Houses. *Japanese Yearbook on Business History*, 13.

Miyamoto, M. (2007). The origins of Japanese-style business management. In M. Miyamoto, T. Abe, M. Udagawa, M. Sawai, and T. Kikkawa, eds., *The Business History of Japan*. Tokyo: Yuhikaku Publishing.

Moore, J. (1993). Predators and prey: A new ecology of competition. *Harvard Business Review*, 71 (May–June), 75–86.

Mowery, D. C., and Teece, D. J. (1993). Japan growing capabilities in industrial-technology: Implications for United States managers and policy-makers. *California Management Review*, 35(2), 9–34.

Mroczkowski, T., and Hanaoka, M. (1989). Continuity and change in Japanese management. *California Management Review*, 31(2), 39–53.

Nambisan, S., and Baron, R. A. (2013). Entrepreneurship in innovation ecosystems: Entrepreneurs' self-regulatory processes and their implications for new venture success. *Entrepreneurship Theory and Practice*, 37(5), 1071–1097.

Namco Networks (2010). Namco Networks' PAC-MAN franchise surpasses 30 million paid transactions in the United States on Brew. Accessed on February 8, 2021, at web.archive.org/web/20170629204316/https://www.businesswire.com/news/home/20100630005033/en/Namco-Networks%E2%80%99-PAC-MAN-Franchise-Surpasses-30-Million.

Noda, K., and Glazer, H. (1968). Traditional Japanese management decision-making. *Management International Review*, 8(2–3), 124–131.

Nonaka, I. (1988). Toward middle-up-down management: Accelerating information creation. *MIT Sloan Management Review*, 29(3), 9–18.

Nonaka, I. (1990). Redundant, overlapping organization: A Japanese approach to managing the innovation process. *California Management Review*, 32(3), 27–38.

Nonaka, I. (1991). The knowledge-creating company. *Harvard Business Review*, 96–104.

Nonaka, I. (1994). A dynamic theory of organizational knowledge creation. *Organization Science*, 5 (1), 14–37.

Nonaka, I. (2011). Introduction. In Kase, K., Slocum, A. and Zhang, Y., *Asian versus Western Management Thinking: Its Culture-Bound Nature*. Basingstoke: Palgrave MacMillan, pp. 1–10.

Nonaka, I., and Johansson, J. K. (1985). Japanese management: What about the hard skills? *Academy of Management Review*, 10(2), 181–191.

Nonaka, I., and Konno, N. (1998). The concept of "Ba": Building a foundation for knowledge creation. *California Management Review*, 40(3), 40–54.

Nonaka, I., and Takeuchi, H. (1995). *The Knowledge-Creating Company: How Japanese Companies Create the Dynamics of Innovation*. Oxford: Oxford University Press.

Nonaka, I. and Takeuchi, H. (2021). Humanizing strategy, *Long Range Planning*, 54(4). DOI: https://doi.org/10.1016/j.lrp.2021.102070.

Nonaka, I., Toyama, R., and Hirata, T. (2008). *Managing Flow: A Process Theory of the Knowledge- Based Firm*. Basingstoke: Palgrave Macmillan.

Nuclear Emergency Response Headquarters (2011). Report of the Japanese Government to the IAEA Ministerial Conference on Nuclear Safety – The Accident at TEPCO's Fukushima Nuclear Power Stations, June 2011, Government of Japan. Accessed on December 31, 2022, at http://flexrisk.boku.ac.at/zitate/full_report.pdf.

Oda, S., and Reynolds, I. (2018). What is womenomics, and is it working for Japan? *Bloomberg*, September 20, 2018. www.bloomberg.com/news/articles/2018-09-19/what-is-womenomics-and-is-itworking-for-japan-quicktake.

Odaka, K. (1986). *Japanese management: A forward looking analysis*. Asian Productivity Organization, Tokyo.

Ogoshi, Y. (2006). Current Japanese employment practices and industrial relations: The transformation of permanent employment and seniority-based wage system. *Asian Business & Management*, 5, 469–485.

Okubayashi, K. (1988). Effect of microelectronics technology in traditional style of management and organization in Japan 2. Kobe University Working Paper No. 9902. January.

Okubayashi, K. (2022). Frontier of Japanese management system going along with IFSAM. In X. Castañer and Y. Zhang-Zhang, eds., *Memory Booklet of 1992 IFSAM Tokyo Congress*. Brussels: International Federation of Scholarly Associations of Management, p. 7.

Okubayashi, K. (1995). Dynamic context of Japanese management. Kobe University Discussion Paper 9501.

Ornatowski, G. K. (1998). The end of Japanese-style human resource management? *MIT Sloan Management Review*, 39(3), 73–85.

Ouchi, W. G. (1981). Theory Z: How American business can meet the Japanese challenge. *Business Horizons*, 24(6), 82–83.

Pascale, R. T. (1978). Personnel practices and employee attitudes: A study of Japanese-managed and American-managed firms in the United States. *Human Relations* 31(7), 597–615.

Pascale, R. T., and Athos, A. G. (1981). *The Art of Japanese Management: Applications for American Executives*. New York: Simon and Schuster.

Paulos, J. A. (2003). *A Mathematician Plays the Stock Market*. New York: Basic Books.

Paumgarten, N. (2010). Master of play. *The New Yorker*, December 12. Accessed on October 28, 2022, at www.newyorker.com/magazine/2010/12/20/master-of-play.

Pilinkienė, V., and Mačiulis, P. (2014). Comparison of different ecosystem analogies: The main economic determinants and levels of impact. *Procedia Social Behavior Science*, 156, 365–370. doi: https//doi.org/10.1016/j.sbspro.2014.11.204

Prochaska, R. J. (1980). Management of innovation in Japan: Why it is successful. *Research Management*, 23(1), 35–38.

Prusak, L. (2000). Where did knowledge management come from? *IBM Systems Journals*, 40(4), 1002–1006.

Pudelko, M. (2004). HRM in Japan and the West: What are the lessons to be learnt from each other? *Asian Business & Management*, 3, 337–361.

Pudelko, M. (2009). The end of Japanese-style management? *Long Range Planning*, 42, 439–462.

Randhawa, K., West, J., Skellern, K., and Josser, E. (2021). Evolving a value chain to an open innovation ecosystem: Cognitive engagement of stakeholders in customizing medical implants. *California Management Review*, 63(2), 101–134.

Rao, B., and Jimenez, B. (2011). A comparative analysis of digital innovation ecosystems. *Proceedings of PICMET Conference – Technology Management in the Energy Smart World*. Portland, Oregon, pp. 1–12.

Ray, T., and Little, S. (2001). Communication and context: Collective tacit knowledge and practice in Japan's workplace *ba*. *Creativity and Innovation Management*, 10(3), 154–164.

Reality Check Team (2018). Reality check: Has Shino Abe's "womenomics" worked in Japan? *BBC News*, February 17, 2018. www.bbc.com/news/worldasia-42993519.

Risjord, M. (2014). *Philosophy of Social Science*. New York: Routledge.

Robinson, A. G., and Schroeder, D. M. (1993). Training, continuous improvement, and human-relations – the United-States TWI programs and the Japanese management style. *California Management Review*, 35(2), 35–57.

Rohlfer, Y., and Zhang, Y. (2016). Cultural studies in international business: Paradigmatic shifts. *European Business Review*, 28(1), 39–62.

Romei, V., and Reed, J. (2019). The Asian century is set to begin. *Financial Times*, March 26. Accessed on March 29, 2019, at www.ft.com/content/520cb6f6-2958-11e9-a5ab-ff8ef2b976c7.

Rong, K. (2011). Nurturing business ecosystem from firm perspectives: Lifecycle, nurturing process, constructs, configuration pattern. PhD thesis. University of Cambridge.

Rothschild, M. L. (1990). *Bionomics: The Inevitability of Capitalism*. New York: H. Holt.

RRBM (2017). Position paper – A vision of responsible research in business and management: Striving for useful and credible knowledge. Community for Responsible Research in Business and Management. https://rrbm.network/wp-content/uploads/2017/11/Position_-Paper.pdf.

Sakikawa, T. (2012). *Transforming Japanese Workplaces*. London and New York: Palgrave MacMillan.

Sakikawa, T. (2019). Japanese management past, present and future directions (日本的経営過去, 現在, その向こう). *Management Science Journal* 経営学論集, 89, 57–66. (In Japanese).

Schodt, F. L. (1983). *Manga! Manga! The World of Japanese Comics*. Tokyo: Kodansha International Ltd.

Sethi, S. P., Namiki, N., and Swanson, C. L. (1984). The decline of the Japanese system of management. *California Management Review*, 26(4), 35–45.

Shanghai Alice Gengaku-dan (2015). Accessed on December 14, 2020, at www16.big.or.jp/~zun/.

Sheff, D. (1993). *Game Over: How Nintendo Zapped an American Industry, Captured Your Dollars, and Enslaved Your Children*. New York: Random House.

Sheff, D. (1999). *Game Over*. Wilton, CT: CyberActive Publishing.

Shibata, T., Baba, Y., Kodama, M., and Suzuki, J. (2019). Managing ambidextrous organizations for corporate transformation: A case study of Fujifilm. *R&D Management*, 49(4), 455–469.

Shikata, N., Goto, S., Gemba, K. (2019). Servitisation of manufacturing industry in Japan. *Forum for Social Economics*, 7(3), 19–30.

Siltaloppi, J., Koskela-Huotari, K., and Vargo, S. L. (2016). Institutional complexity as a driver for innovation in service ecosystems. *Service Science*, 8 (3), 333–343.

Smith, T. M., and Smith, R. L. (2012). *Elements of Ecology*, 8th ed. Boston, MA: Benjamin Cummings.

Soete, L., Verspagen, B., and Weel, B. (2009). *Systems of Innovation*. Maastricht: United Nations University.

Souder, W. E., and Song, X. M. (1998). Analyses of US and Japanese management processes associated with new product success and failure in high and low familiarity markets. *Journal of Product Innovation Management*, 15(3), 208–223.

Spender, J. C. (2013). Nonaka and KM's past, present and future. In G. von Krogh, H. Takeuchi, K. Kase, and C. G. Canton, eds., *Towards Organization Knowledge: The Pioneering Work of Ikujiro Nonaka*. Basingstoke, UK: Palgrave MacMillan, pp. 24–59.

Spender, J. C. (2014). *Business Strategy*. Oxford: Oxford University Press.

Spender, J. C. (2021). The private-sector firm. Presentation at International University of Japan, February 25, 2021.

Startups (2020). About Japan's innovation ecosystem, JETRO. Accessed on Feburary 5, 2022, at www.jetro.go.jp/en/jgc/reports/2020/6790871cde54c518.html.

Statista (2021a). Video game market value worldwide. Accessed on February 24, 2021, at www.statista.com/outlook/dmo/digital-media/video-games/japan.

Statista (2021b). Video games Japan. Accessed on February 24, 2021, at www.statista.com/statistics/292056/video-game-market-value-worldwide/.

Steffensen, S. K. (1998). Informational network industrialization and Japanese business management. *Journal of Organizational Change Management*, 11(6), 515–529.

Sugimoto, Y., and Mouer, R. (1982). *Do the Japanese Fit Their Stereotype?* Tokyo: Tooyoo Keizai.

Sullivan, J. J. (1992). Japanese management philosophies – from the vacuous to the brilliant. *California Management Review*, 34(2), 66–87.

Suseno, Y., and Standing, C. (2018). The systems perspective of national innovation ecosystems. *Systems Research and Behavioral Science*, 35(3), 282–307.

Takeda, K. (2022). Diversity and DX. Seminar at International University of Japan, February 2, 2022.

Takezawa, S., and Whitehill, A. M. (1981). *Workways: Japan and America*. Tokyo: Japan Institute of Labor.

Teece, D. J. (2007). Explicating dynamic capabilities: The nature and microfoundations of (sustainable) enterprise performance. *Strategic Management Journal*, 28(13), 1319–1350.

Teece, D. J. (2008). Foreword: From the management of R&D to knowledge management. Some contributions of Ikujiro Nonaka to the field of strategic management. In I. Nonaka, R. Toyama, and R. Hirata, eds., *Managing Flow: A Process Theory of the Knowledge-Based Firm*. London: Palgrave McMillan, pp. 6–52.

Teece, D. J. (2016). Business Ecosystem. In M. Augier and D. Teece, eds., *The Palgrave Encyclopedia of Strategic Management*. London: Palgrave Macmillan.

Teece, D. J. (2020). Plotting strategy in a dynamic world. *MIT Sloan Management Review*, 62(1), 28–33.

Tsuchiya, T. (1960). *Nihon no Keieisha Seishin [Managerial Mentality in Japan]*. Tokyo: Keizai Oraisha.

Udagawa, M., Hiroki S., Keisuke N., and Izumi N. (1995). The Center for Business and Industrial Research of Hosei University, ed., *Nihon Kigyo no Hinshitsu Kanri* (Quality Control of Japanese enterprises). Tokyo: Yuhikaku Publishing.

Veblen, T. (1915). The opportunity of Japan. *Journal of Race Development*, 6 (1), 23–38.

Warner, M. (1994). Japanese culture, western management: Taylorism and human resources in Japan. *Organization Studies*, 15(4), 509–533.

Warner, M. (2011). Whither Japan? Economy, management and society. *Asia Pacific Business Review*, 17(1), 1–5.

Watanabe, T. (1987). Demystifying Japanese management. Tokyo: Gakuseisha Publishing Co., Ltd.

Westney, E. (2020). Reflecting on Japan's contributions to management theory. *Asian Business & Management*, 19(1), 8–24.

WIPO (2021). World Intellectual Property Indicators 2021. Geneva: World Intellectual Property Organization.

Wood, S. (1990). Tacit skills, the Japanese management model and new technology. *Applied Psychology: An International Review (Psychologie Appliquee: Revue Internationale)*, 39(2), 169–190.

Xie, X., and Wang, H. (2021). How to bridge the gap between innovation niches and exploratory and exploitative innovations in open innovation ecosystems. *Journal of Business Research*, 124, 299–311. https://doi.org/10.1016/j.jbusres.2020.11.058.

Yang, C. Y. (1984). Demystifying Japanese management-practices. *Harvard Business Review*, 62(6), 172–177.

Yoshino, M. Y. (1968). *Japan's Managerial System: Tradition and Innovation*. Cambridge, MA: The Massachusetts Institute of Technology Press.

Zahra, S. A., and Nambisan, S. (2012). Entrepreneurship and strategic thinking in business ecosystems. *Business Horizons*, 55(3), 219–229.

Zarazúa, E. (2021). Fukushima Analysis, nuclear accident that had repercussion at global level. March 11, 2021. https://ibero.mx/prensa/analisis-fukushima-accidente-nuclear-que-tuvo-repercusiones-nivel-global.

Zhang, Y., Dolan, S., Lingham, T., and Altman, Y. (2009). International strategic human resource management: A comparative case analysis of Spanish firms in China. *Management and Organization Review*, 5(2), 195–222.

Zhang, Y., and Zhou, Y. (2015). *The Source of Innovation in China: Highly Innovative Systems*. Basingstoke: Palgrave MacMillan.

Zhang-Zhang, Y., and Kumagai, N. (2020). Women in the workplace: Insights from Japan. IRI Joint Research Series Working Paper (IRI-2020-02), International University of Japan.

Zhang-Zhang, Y., Rohlfer, S., and Rajasekera, J. (2020). An eco-systematic view of cross-sector fintech: The case of Alibaba and Tencent. *Sustainability*, 12, 8907.

Zhang-Zhang, Y., Rohlfer, S., and Varma, A. (2022). Strategic people management in contemporary highly dynamic VUCA contexts: A knowledge worker perspective. *Journal of Business Research*, 144, 587–598.

Zhang-Zhang, Y., and Varma, A. (2020). Organizational preparedness with COVID-19: Strategic planning and human creativity. *The European Business Review*, September–October, 22–33.

Zhang, Y., Zhou, Y., and McKenzie, J. (2013). A humanistic approach to knowledge creation: People centric innovation. In G. von Krogh, H. Takeuchi, K. Kase, and C. G. Canton, eds., *Towards Organization Knowledge: The Pioneering Work of Ikujiro Nonaka*. London: Palgrave MacMillan, pp. 167–189.

Acknowledgments

This Element has been supported by IUJ Research Institute (IRI) Research Grant (grant number IUJ2021-07). The third section (Japanese Character-Based Video Game Industry) of Section 4 is based on a project supported by Japan Society for the Promotion of Science (JSPS) Grant-in-Aid for Scientific Research (19K01926).

The authors wish to express the gratitude to J.-C. Spender, the series editor, for his support and encouragement. We also want to offer thanks to Kiyo Ogushi, Donald Soo, Yukio Takagaki, Haruyoshi Ito, Keita Tsujimoto, Tomoyuki Wada, Ko Fukuda, Hitoshi Nakagami, Shuntaro Hiura, Shohei Hattori, Yosuke Kumagai, Ryosuke Hanada, Shuntaro Asai, Ryotaro Katayama, Okuto Kawakita, Hiroaki Nakakura, and many others for their inspirations. Zanela P. Phiri, Ligia Anceito, and Yuvita Andriana have provided technical support in the research process.

To Nin, for your infinite curiosity and questions of "why". - Yingying

To PhD and Professor Hiroyuki Itami, for your contributions to academia and education. - Kikkawa

Cambridge Elements ≡

Business Strategy

J.-C. Spender
Kozminski University

J.-C. Spender is a research Professor, Kozminski University. He has been active in the business strategy field since 1971 and is the author or co-author of 7 books and numerous papers. His principal academic interest is in knowledge-based theories of the private sector firm, and managing them.

About the Series

Business strategy's reach is vast, and important too since wherever there is business activity there is strategizing. As a field, strategy has a long history from medieval and colonial times to today's developed and developing economies. This series offers a place for interesting and illuminating research including industry and corporate studies, strategizing in service industries, the arts, the public sector, and the new forms of Internet-based commerce. It also covers today's expanding gamut of analytic techniques.

Cambridge Elements ≡

Business Strategy

Elements in the Series

Printed in the United States
by Baker & Taylor Publisher Services